ALCTS Papers on Library Technical Services and Collections, no. 2

Origins, Content, and Future of AACR2 Revised

edited by
Richard P. Smiraglia

series editor
Edward Swanson

American Library Association
Chicago and London 1992

Cover designed by Jim Lange

Text designed by Donavan Vicha, ALA Books, in Times Roman, Helvetica, and Helvetica Narrow, using *Ventura Publisher* 3.0

Printed on 50-pound Glatfelter, a pH-neutral stock, and bound in 10-point C1S stock by Cushing Malloy

The paper used in this publication meets the minimum requirements of American National Standard for Information Sciences—Permanence of Paper for Printed Library Materials, ANSI Z39.48-1984. ∞

Library of Congress Cataloging-in-Publication Data
Origins, content, and future of AACR2 revised / edited by Richard P.
  Smiraglia.
       p.   cm. — (ALCTS papers on library technical services and
  collections ; no. 2)
    Based on papers presented at institutes, called "AACR2 revised, a
  practical update"; sponsored by ALCTS.
    ISBN 0-8389-3405-6
    1. Anglo-American cataloguing rules—Congresses. 2. Descriptive
  cataloging—Rules—Congresses. I. Smiraglia, Richard P., 1952–
  II. Association for Library Collections & Technical Services.
  III. Series.
  Z694.15.A56O75   1992
  025.3′ 2— dc20   91-39734

Printed in the United States of America.

96 95 94 93 92   5 4 3 2 1

Contents

Part Three
A Symposium on the Future

Foreword

Karen Muller

The American Library Association has been involved throughout its existence with the preparation of rules for cataloging. Early proceedings of the Association report decisions on orthography, capitalization, and form of entry, as well as a strong desire to come to agreement on cataloging practices in order to achieve as much economy in the management of libraries as possible.[1] By 1883, the first committee on "cooperation" had prepared its "Condensed Rules for Author and Title Catalog," a short four-page document.[2] The current rules, *Anglo-American Cataloguing Rules,* second edition, not only are much lengthier, but also are published by an international body, the Joint Steering Committee for Revision of AACR. These rules provide for the description of a wide array of library materials, many not even imaginable to our professional predecessors.

Unlike those early "Condensed Rules," our current rules are more than instructions. They are a standard that is based on principles agreed to internationally and that is applied internationally. As Richard Smiraglia and the authors of the papers in *Origins, Content, and Future of AACR2 Revised* note, rule changes are evolutionary. In some ways, this gradual process places a larger burden on each and every cataloger to follow the discussions, understand the principles, and know how to exercise professional judgment in order to describe library materials in such a way that the user can find the desired items.

The provisions of AACR have proved to be applicable to materials in all languages and all formats. As Olivia Madison, Ben Tucker, and Edward Swanson describe, the current rules have been revised to accommodate computer files, compact discs, and popular videorecordings, all formats of library materials that gained popularity in the last decade. Yet catalogers of the last decade did not have to wait for the new instructions in order to add these materials to their libraries. These materials could be described by applying the provisions of the 1978 edition of AACR, and indeed the early efforts contributed greatly to the preparation of the rules for the 1988 revision—just as pioneering librarians today are finding ways to describe interactive video and electronic publications.

The populations libraries serve and the materials libraries house will continue to change. The way in which we describe and make that material accessible also will continue to change. Further, because of the great diversity in purposes of libraries and the wide range in the types of materials that libraries collect, individual catalogers will be faced with descriptive cataloging challenges not yet covered in the rules. The essays in this book provide insights on how the descriptive cataloging challenges of the past have been resolved and point the way for resolving these future issues.

Origins, Content, and Future of AACR2 Revised concludes with a discussion of the future of AACR. With the evolutionary approach to rule revision, there may never be an "AACR3," but the rules we consult in ten years may look very different. Work is currently underway to allow for a machine-readable version of AACR to be developed and licensed for library workstation applications. Using and applying the rules in an interactive mode, much as the user of the catalog will use an online catalog, will result in new approaches to bibliographic organization. If the discussions of the past are any indicator of the future, the basic principles will remain the same and will be part of the cataloging standards continuum that is as old as our profession.

Notes

1. See, for example, the reports of the 1887 ALA Conference, *Library Journal* 12 (1887): 413–35, and of the 1888 Conference, *Library Journal* 13 (1888): 321–22.
2. American Library Association, Cooperation Committee, "Condensed Rules for an Author and Title Catalog," *Library Journal* 8 (1883): 251–54.

Introduction

Richard P. Smiraglia

Late in 1988 a revised text of the *Anglo-American Cataloguing Rules,* second edition (AACR2), was quietly published. In stark contrast to the events surrounding the initial appearance of AACR2 in 1978, there was no need for a massive professional re-education program, there were no implementation cost studies, and there was relatively little anxiety among catalogers anticipating the arrival of the new volume. The articles in this volume celebrate the publication of the 1988 revision of AACR2, referred to hereafter as AACR2R.

To mark the 1988 event, the Committee on Cataloging: Description and Access (CC:DA) of the Cataloging and Classification Section, Resources and Technical Services Division (now Association for Library Collections & Technical Services (ALCTS)), American Library Association, sponsored a program session, "AACR2 Revised: Past, Present and Future," at the 1988 ALA Annual Conference. The session featured three presentations that were designed to "provide information on the origin and content of the revised version, the international cooperation that has resulted in continuous revision of AACR2, and possible future developments."[1]

During the year following the publication of AACR2R, ALCTS presented a series of regional institutes called "AACR2 Revised: A Practical Update." In these sessions, participants were given a thorough overview of the basic precepts of descriptive cataloging as well as the revised portions of the code. The papers from the earlier conference program, revised somewhat, served as the basis for plenary sessions at these institutes, with the addition of a formal presentation on rule interpretation. Interspersed between plenary sessions were workshop presentations on description of monographs, manuscripts, and serials (or, the bibliographic conditions), description of nonbook materials, and choice and form of access points. The material presented at the institutes forms the basis of the contents of this volume.

In this brief introduction, the nature of AACR2 is explored to set the context for the papers that make up this volume, which are subsequently described.

What Is AACR2?

Obviously, there are several answers to such a question. For most catalogers, AACR2 is the set of current rules for compiling descriptions and for choosing and formulating access points. In other words, AACR2 provides the guidelines by which descriptive cataloging is accomplished.

AACR2 is the latest successor to a long Anglo-American tradition of descriptive cataloging. This tradition stems from Anthony Panizzi's 91 rules for the British Museum catalog issued in 1841. These rules were subsequently reformulated by Charles C. Jewett in 1852 for the Smithsonian Institution catalog. Practices derived from these rules were refined by Charles A. Cutter and, couched among statements of principle, published in his *Rules for a Dictionary Catalog* in 1876. AACR2 follows nearly a century of formal Anglo-American cooperation that began with the publication of the first joint code in 1908.[2]

More recent influences are also evident. Incorporating the legacies of Andrew Osborn and Seymour Lubetzky, AACR2 represents a valiant attempt to produce a pragmatic code, that is, a code in which rules are relatively few and simple and catalogers are expected to rely on their professional judgment as individual cases demand. This approach arose in response to the crisis in cataloging that by the 1950s had brought an end to what Osborn, in his famous 1941 article, had termed an era of legalism, in which rules were devised to cover every situation that arose.[3]

The crisis was uncovered in the 1940s when it was discovered that the Library of Congress (LC) had an arrearage of 1,670,161 volumes out of a total estimated collection of 5.8 million volumes, and that the arrearage was increasing at the rate of 30,000 volumes per year.[4] Martha Yee has pointed out the important role of cataloging education, or rather the lack of it, in the development of this crisis by noting that LC's large cataloging department employed many nonprofessionals and suggesting that "some of the legalistic approach might have been an attempt to turn cataloging into a set of procedures that could be followed by low-level or untrained staff without professional judgment."[5]

To develop a pragmatic approach to cataloging, Seymour Lubetzky was engaged to discover the essentials of the complex rules that existed at that time. Lubetzky's clarion call—"Is this rule necessary?"—has become a fixture in code revision circles.[6]

AACR2 is a pragmatic code. Its rules are broad guidelines that embody solid principles and are intended to be applied by professional people exercising their own bibliographic judgment as individual cases demand. The rules in this particular code must be applicable to all kinds of works in all sorts of physical manifestations, which must be described for a variety of catalogs used by all levels of users in many different types of libraries. AACR2 represents a significant contribution to the growth of cataloging principles.

AACR2 is also one cog in the international wheel of universal bibliographic control. Based on agreements embodied in the decisions of the International Conference on Cataloguing Principles in 1961 and incorporating the International Standards for Bibliographic Description, AACR2 is an important partner in the international effort to share bibliographic data.

AACR2 is an important literary property and a best-selling book. ALA sold 87,574 copies of AACR2 and, as of this writing, 54,250 copies of AACR2R have been sold.[7] In addition to the standard text that is used in all English-speaking countries, translations have been authorized or published in Arabic, Finnish, French, Japanese, Korean, Malaysian, Norwegian, Portuguese, Spanish, Swedish, and Urdu.[8] Because AACR2 is a book, grammar, spelling, typesetting, indexing, etc., are all important aspects of its production. The glossary, for example, is careful to define only terms used in the text in some way that is peculiar to that text. Stylistically, all rules are written in the imperative.

The 1988 Revision

What exactly is the 1988 revision? Is it a new edition of the rules, a new code, a mere reprinting? As usual, the answer is complex.

Like its predecessors, AACR2 has undergone constant revision. Three packets of revisions were published between 1978 and 1985. Further revisions, agreed to following the publication of the 1985 revision packet, needed to be incorporated. The revisions taken together can be seen to incorporate refinements of some of AACR2's innovations as well as some entirely new provisions.

These revisions stand as a tribute to the process of continuous revision that began officially with the publication of AACR2. They represent nearly a decade of thoughtful refinements of principles already present in the code. While none may be remembered as milestones in cataloging history, taken together they clearly constitute a significant change from the provisions of the 1978 publication.

Elsewhere I have argued that these changes constitute a new edition, at least in the technical sense of the word.[9] Gorman has quite rightly pointed out that the revision does not represent a professionally wrenching paradigm shift and that it is entirely appropriate to refrain from calling it AACR3.[10] In a sense, we are both correct. It seems perfectly logical to conceptualize the 1967, 1978, and 1988 publications as representing roughly equivalent nodes on a bibliographic continuum. That is, each incorporates principles and framework agreed to internationally, each represents a refinement of those agreements, and each incorporates extensions of those provisions to new or evolving communications media.

Yet, the full implementation of the 1978 version of AACR2 caused a tremendous shift in the descriptive cataloging paradigm, largely because of the incomplete implementation of its 1967 predecessor. Because the revision process has been continuous, and changes have been implemented gradually over the past decade, no such drastic shift has occurred as a result of the publication of AACR2R. Whatever we choose to call the new volume, it remains a tribute to the process of continuous revision. In a sense it is the proof of the success of that process.

Papers in This Volume

This volume is organized in three parts. The articles in Part 1 provide contextual information about AACR2R, its origin, and the process by which it came to be published. Adaptations of cataloging workshop presentations, in which the specific content of AACR2R is covered, constitute Part 2. Part 3 is a symposium on the future of descriptive cataloging and AACR.

Part 1 opens with "A Summary of Changes in AACR2 Revised" by Olivia M. A. Madison, in which the major differences between AACR2 and AACR2R are described. Madison neatly categorizes the changes as editorial revisions, expansion of provisions already in the code, and actual changes to the code. Richard P. Smiraglia describes "The Continuous Revision Process" by which AACR2 evolves. The representative process is deliberately complex and circuitous to assure broad support for the rules and to prevent jarring change. To balance Madison and Smiraglia's North American overview of rule revision, Elaine Hall's "The Third 'A' on JSCAACR" describes her experiences as Australia's representative to the

Joint Steering Committee for Revision of AACR. Part 1 ends with "AACR2: Implementation and Interpretation of 1988 Revision" by Ben R. Tucker, in which the role of the Library of Congress as purveyor and arbiter of the rules is described.

Part 2 contains four chapters, adapted from cataloging workshops by the ALCTS institute faculty, in which specific rule changes in AACR2 are detailed. These chapters cover general bibliographic description by Olivia M. A. Madison; description of nonbook materials by Ben R. Tucker and Edward Swanson; description of computer files by Edward Swanson; and choice and form of access points by Carlen Ruschoff.

Part 3 is a symposium on the future of descriptive cataloging and AACR2. The lead article is "After AACR2R: The Future of the *Anglo-American Cataloguing Rules*" by Michael Gorman, editor of AACR2R, author of *The Concise AACR2, 1988 Revision,* and prominent library visionary. Gorman's presentation is accompanied by responses prepared by Michael Carpenter, Sheila Intner, Pat Thomas, Barbara Tillett, and Arnold Wajenberg. These five experts in descriptive cataloging state their own visions for the future, to each of which Gorman responds briefly.

Conclusion

Several points emerge and are reiterated throughout the three segments of this volume. Probably most important is the dichotomous entity that AACR2R represents for the cataloging community. That is, it is a landmark work precisely because it does not constitute a major shift in cataloging. AACR2R achieves this status as a result of the representative revision process, which is sensitive to changing communication technologies, as well as changing needs in the cataloging community and among library users worldwide.

However, it is clear that the future holds even greater potential. Bibliographic control in general, descriptive cataloging in particular, and even the *Anglo-American Cataloguing Rules,* must change in order to remain effective as tools for the exploitation of recorded knowledge.

Notes

1. American Library Association, *1988 ALA Conference Program—New Orleans* (Chicago: American Library Association, 1988), 158.
2. This history is carefully portrayed in articles by Ruth French Strout, "The Development of the Catalog and Cataloging Codes," *Library Quarterly* 26 (Oct. 1956): 254–75; and Kathryn Luther Henderson, " 'With a Degree of Uniformity and

Common Sense': Descriptive Cataloging in the United States, 1876–1975," *Library Trends* 25 (July 1976): 227–71.

3. Andrew Osborn, "The Crisis in Cataloging," *Library Quarterly* 11 (Oct. 1941): 393–411.

4. *Annual Report of the Librarian of Congress for the Fiscal Year Ended June 30, 1940.* (Washington, D.C.: Library of Congress, 1940), 11.

5. Martha Yee, "Attempts to Deal with the 'Crisis in Cataloging' at the Library of Congress in the 1940s," *Library Quarterly* 57 (Jan. 1987): 19.

6. Seymour Lubetzky, *Cataloging Rules and Principles* (Washington, D.C.: Library of Congress, 1953), 3.

7. Figures for 1978 ed. final as of Sept. 30, 1987 (telephone conversation with Karen Muller, Executive Director, Resources and Technical Services Division, Oct. 19, 1987). Figures for 1988 ed. final as of April 30, 1991 (telephone conversation with Evelyn Shaevel, Director of Marketing, ALA Publishing, June 3, 1991).

8. Muller conversation; supplemented by telephone conversations with Helen F. Schmierer, ALA Representative to the Joint Steering Committee, Oct. 22, 1987, and with Evelyn Shaevel, Director of Marketing, ALA Publishing, June 3, 1991.

9. Richard P. Smiraglia, "The Consolidated Reprinting of AACR2," Guest editorial, *Cataloging and Classification Quarterly* 8 (1987): 3–6. The volume constitutes a new edition, in the sense that it represents a new impression with significant textual alterations.

10. Michael Gorman, "Call It AACR2 1/2, or Après la guerre, or Daughter of a Dynamic Decade," *American Libraries* 19 (May 1988): 387–88.

Contributors to This Volume

Michael Carpenter is an assistant professor at the School of Library and Information Science, Louisiana State University. He has served as a voting member of the ALA Committee on Cataloging: Description and Access (CC:DA) since 1988. He is the author of *Corporate Authorship* (Greenwood Press, 1981) and the editor of *Foundations of Cataloging* (Libraries Unlimited, 1985) and *National and International Bibliographic Databases* (Haworth Press, 1988).

Michael Gorman is dean of library services, California State University, Fresno. He is the co-editor of the *Anglo-American Cataloguing Rules*, second edition, and the *Anglo-American Cataloguing Rules*, second edition, 1988 revision, and the author of *The Concise AACR2* and *The Concise AACR2, 1988 Revision*, among other works.

Elaine Hall is manager, collection development, at the National Library of New Zealand. She previously served as the deputy cataloguing librarian and as the manager, extension services, at the State Library of New South Wales. In 1981 she was appointed a foundation member of the Australian Committee on Cataloguing and the Australian Bibliographic Network Standards Committee and served on those committees until 1989 and 1986 respectively. From 1984 to 1989 she was the Australian representative on the Joint Steering Committee for Revision of AACR.

Sheila S. Intner is a professor at Simmons College Graduate School of Library and Information Science. She served as the chair of the Cataloging and Classification Section of the Resources and Technical Services Division of ALA, 1989–90, and as editor of *Library Resources & Technical Services,* 1987–90. She is the author of numerous books and articles, including *Standard Cataloging for School and Public Libraries* (Libraries Unlimited, 1990) and *Cataloging, the Professional Development Cycle* (Greenwood Press, 1991). She currently is the editor of the Frontiers of Access to Library Materials series for ALA Books.

Olivia M. A. Madison has just been appointed assistant director for public services at Iowa State University, following six years as head of the cataloging department. From 1981 to 1985 she was a voting member of CC:DA and served as chair of the committee, 1984–85.

Karen Muller is the executive director of the Association for Library Collections & Technical Services. From 1982 to 1985 she was the Art Libraries Society of North America representative to CC:DA.

Carlen Ruschoff is head, cataloging department, Georgetown University Library. She served as a voting member of CC:DA from 1984 to 1988 and was secretary of the committee, 1986–88. Since 1988 she has served as chair of the planning committee for the ALCTS institutes on the 1988 revision of AACR2.

Richard P. Smiraglia is an assistant professor, School of Library Service, Columbia University. He served as a member of CC:DA from 1980 to 1988, first as the Music Library Association representative, then as a voting member, 1984–88, and as chair, 1986–88. He is the editor of *Library Resources & Technical Services* (1990–) and of the Music Library Association's *Technical Reports Series*. He is the author of numerous books, including *Music Cataloging* (Libraries Unlimited, 1989) and *Cataloging Music,* 2d ed. (Soldier Creek Press, 1987), and the editor of *Describing Archival Materials* (Haworth Press, 1990).

Edward Swanson is principal cataloger, Minnesota Historical Society. He has served as a voting member of CC:DA from 1979 to 1983 and from 1990 to the present, and as chair of the committee from 1990. He also has served as a member of the interdivisional MARBI Committee from 1973 to 1977, and as a member of the OCLC Cataloging Advisory Committee and the OCLC Cataloging and Database Services Advisory Committee from 1979 to 1990. He is a frequent instructor and author on cataloging, and serves as editor in chief for Soldier Creek Press and as editor of the ALCTS Papers on Library Technical Services and Collections series.

Pat Thomas is head cataloger, Stockton-San Joaquin County Public Library. She was a voting member of CC:DA from 1980 to 1984 and served as chair of the committee, 1983–84.

Barbara B. Tillett is head of cataloging, Central University Library, University of California, San Diego. As a teacher, researcher, writer, and practitioner, she has focused on cataloging concerns, including authority control, bibliographic relationships, "multiple versions," and automated systems.

Ben R. Tucker is the chief of the Office for Descriptive Cataloging Policy at the Library of Congress. He serves as the Library of Congress member of the Joint Steering Committee for Revision of AACR, which he chaired from 1989 to 1991. He also is the Library of Congress representative to CC:DA.

Arnold Wajenberg is principal cataloger, University of Illinois at Urbana-Champaign. He served as a voting member of CC:DA from 1982 to 1986 and currently is a member of the OCLC Cataloging and Database Services Advisory Committee and of the Dewey Decimal Classification Editorial Policy Committee.

A Summary of Changes in AACR2 Revised

Olivia M. A. Madison

In January 1981, when the Library of Congress (LC) and the majority of the American cataloging community formally implemented AACR2, catalogers had read a myriad of review articles of all persuasions, heard countless dire implementation predictions, and participated in untold numbers of workshops and institutes. AACR2 influenced the very foundation of how we in the United States create and evaluate our catalogs. Also, it is easy to forget that there were similar concerns throughout the Anglo-American cataloging community, as AACR2 truly merged what had been separate British and American cataloging codes. The code's "author," the Joint Steering Committee for Revision of AACR (JSC), was composed originally of representatives from the United States, Canada, and Great Britain. A fourth country, Australia, is now represented as well. Furthermore, as stated in the 1988 revision of AACR2, the code generally has been adopted in most English-speaking countries and has been or is being translated into many foreign languages.[1]

As soon as AACR2 was published there were calls not only to begin rule revision but also to begin planning for AACR3. In March 1981, Charles Martell wrote that "a simple charting of the history of modern code revisions gives a trend that suggests revisions at an increasing rapid rate ... [and]

Throughout this volume the first edition of *Anglo-American Cataloguing Rules* will be referred to as AACR or AACR1; the second edition is referred to as AACR2; and the revision of the second edition as AACR2R.

that the next code revision is due between 1983 and 1988."[2] With this initial backdrop, apparently the JSC was uncertain as to its role regarding rule revision. At its June 1981 meeting, the American Library Association's Committee on Cataloging: Description and Access (CC:DA) discussed and affirmed to ALA's JSC representative, Frances Hinton, its support for rule revision where it was obviously needed and desired.[3] Furthermore, at this CC:DA meeting the question arose whether or not "a revised edition of the code bore discussion." This question was met with groans of dismay.[4] With guidance from its constituent groups, the JSC at its August 1981 meeting chose to move ahead with rule revision, thus laying the groundwork for the eventuality of a revised code, not a new edition.[5]

The primary purpose of this article is to describe the major differences between AACR2 as originally published and the 1988 revision (AACR2R). In order to provide a framework for the major changes that were made, some early criticism of the code is briefly reviewed. This is followed by a cursory description of the types of changes that have been made, together with examples of those changes. Two substantive revisions that appear in AACR2R, those concerning the rules for pseudonyms and those for computer files, are explained in greater detail. Personal observations on the revised code and on the evolutionary process of code revision conclude this article.

Early Criticism of AACR2

It is useful to review the context from which these rule revisions emerged, that is, the early negative criticism of AACR2. Some of these early objections to provisions in the rules were shown to be real problems during the rule revision process, others emerged as Library of Congress rule interpretations, and the rest might or might not remain problems, however dormant.

Much of the outcry concerning AACR2 regarded its implementation, rather than the code itself. In particular, there was great concern about the potential effect of the new rules on card catalogs. Because libraries anticipated massive numbers of name heading changes and many were not able or willing to change those headings, they were faced with what was known as "closing" their catalogs. These "closings" were common because at the time few libraries had online catalogs with sophisticated maintenance systems. Instead, the majority had very labor-intensive manual maintenance systems, which for heading changes involved changing catalog entry cards and recording the new authenticated forms of headings. While LC initially was interested in implementing AACR2 in January 1980, the Association of Research Libraries was instrumental in leading the drive to delay implementation for one year. The reasons for this delay were the financial and training implications of local (that is, non-LC) implementation.[6]

One very public and heated disagreement concerned AACR2's treatment of microform reproductions of printed works. In fact, this is still a controversial topic. AACR2's approach was a radical departure from that of the 1967 edition of the *Anglo-American Cataloging Rules* (AACR). Under AACR, descriptions of microform reproductions were created to reflect details of the original publications with subordinate microform descriptions given in the notes areas. AACR2, with its emphasis on the item in hand, called for the reverse: microforms were to be described to reflect details of the microform with subordinate descriptions of the original publication given in the notes area. In January 1980, because of open public dissatisfaction with these rules, CC:DA formed a task force to respond to the objections raised. In February 1981 CC:DA held public hearings on the topic where individuals spoke for and against AACR2's provisions. There was no broad consensus on any of the alternatives.[7] Four months later, in June 1981, a divided CC:DA supported LC's practical solution, in which the primary description was to reflect details of the original publication, but in AACR2 format. When the JSC considered the issue in July 1981, it chose not to take action because it concluded that the issues had not been thoroughly discussed by all of its constituent groups. Ten years later the cataloging community is still debating the way microform reproductions should be cataloged.

Other objections were raised as well. Controversy arose over AACR2's compromise treatment for persons writing under more than one name, a treatment that appeared to satisfy no one. AACR2's elimination of corporate authorship and constriction of main entry under corporate body headings, and the subsequent increase of serial title main entries, were strongly objected to on philosophical grounds by C. Sumner Spalding and others.[8]

Some reviewers deplored the liberal use of optional rules, and others were distressed over the rules governing corporate body headings. Catalogers in the music, serial, and computer file communities expressed concern over their respective chapters' ambiguities and problems with their implementations of the rules. The negative reviews of the 1978 code should not be overly exaggerated, because there was an abundance of positive support; however, rule revision evolves out of dissatisfaction.

Revisions: An Overview

There is no doubt that the JSC has taken its rule revision role seriously. The JSC began to issue annual rule revision packets in 1982, and those annual revision packets eventually led to the publication of AACR2R. For the purposes of this discussion, rule revisions in AACR2R can be seen to fall into the following three categories:

1. simplification and editorial revisions;
2. expansion of provisions already in the code; and,
3. changes to the code.

In the discussion that follows, no attempt is made to list all revisions. Rather, representative revisions will be discussed for illustration.

Simplification and Editorial Revisions

Rule 1.5B4. Playing time for sound recordings, motion pictures, etc., now is based on what is stated on the item. Previously, playing time was given in minutes, rounded to the next minute up.

Rules 25.25–25.35. The rules for formulating uniform titles for musical works have been reorganized so that they now appear in the order used to construct these headings.

Expansion

Glossary. New glossary terms have been included; decisions to add glossary terms are based on JSC guidelines approved in 1984.

Chapter 9, Computer Files. Chapter 9 is greatly expanded.

Area 5 and GMD. Area 5 (physical description area) and general material designation (GMD) are expanded throughout the chapters in Part I to include descriptions for braille and other raised type and for large-print materials.

Rule 4.2. Instructions for "edition" statements that identify versions of manuscripts are included.

Changes to the Code

Prescribed Sources of Information. The prescribed sources of information for series and for the serial title proper (found at rules 2.0B2 and 12.0B) are changed and made parallel. For series in books there is a clear hierarchy of choices. The choices begin with the series title page; AACR2 used the entire publication. For serials, the analytical title page is now the first preference as a title page substitute. AACR2 used the cover as the first preference.

Rules 21.2A and 21.2C. The new instructions for recognizing serial title changes further limit the instances of such title changes.

Rules 22.2C2 and 22.2C3. Instructions for headings for authors who write under more than one name are changed.

Rule 23.4D. British place names are qualified by England, Scotland, Wales, and Ireland, instead of by the county name.

Two Revisions in Detail

Although AACR2R contains many different types of revisions, two revisions are of particular interest because they have such substantial potential effect on our catalogs. These two revisions are the new rules for entry of persons writing under pseudonyms, which will have great impact on personal name heading files, and the new rules for description of computer files, which were designed to accommodate an important new type of library material. Also, these revisions clearly demonstrate the potential complexities of, and the length of time necessary for, the rule revision process.

Pseudonyms

Perhaps the initial commentary and final rule revision for pseudonyms best epitomize the controversy surrounding the 1978 edition. Upon publication, AACR2 was criticized for its lack of a theoretical base and for its pragmatic approach towards the catalog as a finding tool. AACR, with its stated purpose of meeting "the needs of general research libraries," had required that in the case of an author who published under his or her own name and at least one pseudonym, or under multiple pseudonyms, catalogers enter the author under the name by which he or she was primarily identified in modern editions of his or her works or in reference sources.[9] In case of doubt, AACR instructed catalogers to prefer the real name. AACR also provided an alternative rule for entering such authors under the names appearing in their respective works with "see also" cross references linking the various names. AACR2 coupled these two separate AACR instructions. First, in rule 22.2C2, the cataloger was asked to determine predominance of use of multiple names and to use the predominant form as the heading. Then, in rule 22.2C3, if no predominance could be determined, the cataloger was instructed to use the name appearing in each item as a legitimate heading.[10]

Clearly the transition to a generalized approach from the research-oriented approach of AACR can be seen in these two rules. However, the obvious attempt at compromise in AACR2 had satisfied no one.

Individuals favoring the creation of headings for all names used by authors who write under pseudonyms were not satisfied by the direction to first attempt to establish predominance. Sanford Berman, a speaker and commentator at the ALA Information Science and Automation Division's Institutes on the Catalog, stated that:

> All pseudonyms should be legitimized. If an author chooses to write a book as Jean Plaidy, and the publisher not only prints "Jean Plaidy" on the title page but also advertises and markets the book that way, and reviewers review it that way, and bookstores sell it that way, and patrons expect to find it shelved that way, how does it serve either findability or common sense to catalog it under Hibbert?[11]

At the other end of the spectrum, disagreement arose over the use of more than one heading to represent the works of any individual author. John Duke criticized rule 22.2C because he said it weakened the second of Seymour Lubetzky's objectives of a catalog, that being to relate and display the editions that a library has of a given work and the works it has by a given author.[12] Although the obvious advantage of rule 22.2C3 is that it meets the needs of a person looking for a book written under a particular name, Duke believed that this rule would hamper persons interested in examining all works by an author and concluded that "the solution is clear—abandon the rule and substitute one form of name with the needed references for each author."[13] Bruce Ford, while applauding AACR2's attempt to resolve many of the prior conflicts surrounding the role of the catalog as stated by Charles A. Cutter and later restated by Seymour Lubetzky, castigated the two rules regarding pseudonyms and called them "nebulous and threatening to standardization."[14]

Confusion arose over AACR2's attempt to incorporate the need for predominance of name usage as well as to introduce the use of pseudonyms. Following the publication of AACR2, there was much discussion of and confusion concerning how to determine predominance and at what stage it could be decided that there was no predominance. Over time, controversy about these two rules abated and LC issued various rule interpretations regarding their use. No rule revision proposal emerged until the spring of 1985. When it came, the rule revision proposal came from a most surprising source.

By the early spring of 1985, the JSC had considered approximately two hundred rule revision proposals from its constituent members and the editors of AACR2. The Library of Congress had submitted its sixty-eighth proposal, CC:DA its fortieth, and the Canadian Committee on Cataloging its fifty-seventh. Then, from the Land Down Under came the first rule revision proposal from the Australian JSC representative. While the Australians had had a JSC representative for four years, they had never before proposed a rule revision. This proposal was, no less, the abolishment of rule 22.2C2 and the reaffirmation of the principles of rule 22.2C3. The Australians proposed that if a person uses multiple pseudonyms (or his or her real name and one or more pseudonyms), one should choose as the basis of the heading for each item the name appearing in it, and make references to connect the names.

At its July 1985 meeting, CC:DA quickly established a task force to study the Australian pseudonym proposal. Ultimately CC:DA recommended to the JSC that it approve the concept of bibliographic identities, proposed initially by Michael Gorman. Further, CC:DA recommended that the revised instructions be limited to current fiction, but not limited to English-language fiction, and that the current text of rule 22.2C2 be dropped and the following text be substituted for rule 22.2C3: "If a contemporary author uses more than one pseudonym, or his own name and a pseudonym, use as the basis for the heading for each work the name appearing in it." [15]

The JSC completed its discussion on the Australian pseudonym proposal at its London meeting in October 1986. It agreed to drop the predominance instruction in rule 22.2C2; therefore, the frequency of the form found on chief sources of works by the author no longer would be a component decision. The JSC also restricted the use of rule 22.2C3 to authors with separate bibliographical identities or those who are contemporary.[16]

Chapter 9. Computer Files

Perhaps no revision better illustrates the role of the JSC in expansionary rule revision and the evolutionary nature of AACR2 than the revised rules for computer files contained in chapter 9. These rules are indicative of the desire to avoid drastic rule changes. This is, of course, wise hindsight because it was very unclear at the January 1983 CC:DA meeting in San Antonio that the process would work.

It took very little time following the implementation of AACR2 for catalogers to identify problems with the application of chapter 9. In 1981 the International Association of Social Science Information Services and

Technology forwarded to CC:DA a series of recommendations on chapter 9 rule revision. Ultimately, CC:DA forwarded to the JSC fourteen rule revision proposals and a series of recommended additions to the AACR2 glossary. Most of these rule revision proposals involved changes to file description, identification of the chief source of information, the role of producers, and the definition of "dataset" name.

The JSC discussed the CC:DA proposals at its September 1982 meeting and recommended that many of the CC:DA concerns could best be met by a CC:DA-written manual on cataloging for what were then called machine-readable data files (MRDF).[17] The resulting heated debate at the January 1983 CC:DA meeting centered on whether or not the JSC was interested in revising rules and adding terms to the glossary. Nancy John, the CC:DA chair, noted that CC:DA had voted in 1981 to support the process of revising rules as needed and that the chapter 9 rules were an example of a whole block of rules that did not cover fully a developing type of material.[18] Ultimately, CC:DA resubmitted its proposals, and the JSC did consider them fully, with the outcome being rule revision.

CC:DA also was faced with growing frustrations of catalogers who were attempting to apply chapter 9 to a new type of machine-readable material, microcomputer software. Convincing letters from Ben R. Tucker,[19] the LC CC:DA representative, and Glenn Patton,[20] the OCLC CC:DA representative, urged CC:DA to establish a task force to write guidelines addressing the application of chapter 9 to microcomputer software. It was clear to CC:DA that chapter 9, as originally written, was designed to describe dynamic machine-readable data files and not self-contained commercial software packages. While CC:DA was not interested in writing a complete MRDF cataloging manual, it did wish to provide guidance for the cataloging of microcomputer software vis-à-vis chapter 9. Therefore, it established a MRDF task force with Ben Tucker serving as chair and Arnold Wajenberg as the assistant chair.

CC:DA documentation and the numerous articles written on the subject of AACR2 and microcomputer software clearly indicate that cataloging rules for microcomputer software were a subject of broad-based and strong feelings. The consensus was clear to all concerned—revision was a necessity. Some of the most eminent catalogers in this field entered the debate. All had variant approaches regarding some aspects of the required revision. Two years later, in January 1984, CC:DA acted upon its task force's proposed guidelines. The American Library Association then quickly published the guidelines later that year.[21] As could have been expected, much discussion followed the publication of the guidelines. The JSC then began earnest deliberations on the acknowledged need for revision to accommodate microcomputer software, using both CC:DA's guidelines and a corresponding British document. After the JSC completed its preliminary work on chapter 9 rule revision, it published a "finalized" draft a year before the planned publication of AACR2R because it wanted to "bridge the gap between the rules a library may be using . . . and the eventual publication of the final version in 1988."[22]

While the final JSC revision of chapter 9 contains many changes to the original rules, much of the substantive revision centers on four general areas:

1. chief source of information;
2. general material designation;
3. file characteristics and file description areas; and,
4. notes for system requirements.

Chief Source of Information

AACR2 prescribed use of an internal user label as the chief source of information, which caused much confusion. According to Sue Dodd, the usual interpretation of the term "internal user label" has been that of "an 'internal' user header label," a rarely used optional standard for magnetic tapes.[23] Dodd also pointed out that user labels are not always compatible. Because different computers use different operating systems, the labeling devices are often incompatible; therefore, many systems simply bypass labeled tapes.[24]

In early 1982, CC:DA recommended in its second rule revision proposal for chapter 9 that a footnote be added to rule 9.0B1 stating "that at the time these rules were issued, creation of user labels had been an option for labeled tapes, but not a widespread practice."[25] While CC:DA supported the principle that the item itself or some part of it should serve as the chief source of information, it recognized that user labels had not gained the acceptance that had been anticipated during the writing of AACR2. Now the revised chapter 9 states that the chief source of information is to be the title screen. In the end, the intent of AACR2—that the item itself should be used as the preferred chief source of information—was carried out in the revised chapter 9, and the text has been revised to remove the inappropriate term "internal user label." The revised rules also changed the order and types of alternative preferable sources of information and instructed that the source of the title be given in a note.

General Material Designation

The general material designation (GMD) became the source of great concern for cataloging computer file material—probably because the original GMD, "machine-readable data file," was so cumbersome and inaccurate. Complaints centered on the fact that data files are only one kind of machine-readable material, programs being another. At the time other GMD suggestions included "microcomputer software," "computer software," "machine-readable file," and "computer material." The JSC finally settled on "computer file." The intensity of the GMD debate no doubt reflects catalogers' great concern over what appears so early in the display of bibliographic descriptions.

File Characteristics and File Description Areas: Areas 3 and 5

Normally the various area 5s in AACR2 describe the physical characteristics of items being cataloged. However, chapter 9's original area 5 instructed that the file characteristics, rather than the physical carrier, be described. At the time AACR2 was written, the importance of the physical nature was moot because access to computer files was usually through mainframe computers, and often the physical format of these files changed over time. For example, the format could change from punched cards at one stage to magnetic tape at another stage. Therefore the bibliographic importance of this type of file was its content, not its physical format. Microcomputer software changed the rules of the game because these computer files are contained in stable physical carriers and are not as likely to change. There were strong proponents for both physical and content descriptions. While the CC:DA guidelines instructed that both descriptions were to be given in area 5, the revised chapter 9 has split the two descriptions into two different areas. Area 3 is now the file characteristics area, which gives the type of file (e.g., Computer program) followed by the file content description. Area 5 is a true physical description area for those computer files with physical carriers. For those files available only through remote computer access, physical descriptions are not given. The final solution is similar in concept to the rules used for serial descriptions, and it provides a continuity in practical application.

Notes for System Requirements

With the introduction of microcomputer software, which can run only on specified types of hardware, the JSC was urged to include a system requirements note in chapter 9's revisions. The JSC agreed, and the rules now require such a note.

Example:

```
System requirements: IBM PC or IBM PC
    compatible; 128K; DOS 1.1 to DOS 2.1.
```

Conclusion

While some may argue that AACR2R is in actuality a new edition, I would say that it is not. While the code has undergone editorial revisions, expansion, and rule changes, it has not undergone a fundamental change from its original principles. In fact, the revisions bring it closer to those principles, namely:

1. an emphasis on the item in hand;
2. a practical approach towards the art of cataloging; and,
3. a pragmatic view of the catalog as a finding tool.

This is an amazing achievement. In a 1985 survey of library educators and experienced catalogers, Nurieh Mesavi found both groups adamantly opposed to the development of a code that would be a radical departure from the principles of AACR2.[26] Much of the concern regarding AACR2 in the late 1970s related to its costly implementation, both in terms of training and its effects on local card catalogs and national bibliographic databases. Any fundamental changes to the code would meet with extreme resistance, in large part because libraries have constantly dwindling resources that could be directed to implement such changes.

The process of AACR rule revision is long and complicated. It involves an incredible number of individuals and groups, with untold hours of effort and major financial resources. Obviously at the center of this revision is the JSC, and the success of AACR as an international cataloging code rests with it. The JSC, as an author, proved itself practical, forward thinking, and open to reexamining its previous decisions. While there always will be professional debate within the JSC over rule revision proposals in large part because of the JSC's international composition, the ultimate strength of AACR code revision is consensus building. The only time during the years of rule revision culminating in AACR2R that there appeared to have been a potential breakdown of such consensus was during the JSC deliberations over proposed changes to type 3 of general corporate body and government body headings. Ultimately the issues regarding type 3 were worked out.

In 1978, when AACR2 was first published, some prophesied that it was only a minor step towards AACR3, a prediction that has not been fulfilled.

Clearly AACR2R does not meet every need and expectation for bibliographic control; this is to be expected from a general, international, cataloging code. The code continues along its original path as a practical cataloging tool with an emphasis on the item in hand; therein lies its success. The strong agreements for cooperative bibliographic efforts both within the United States and internationally have extended the viability of this cataloging code and have led to this discussion of AACR2R.

Notes

1. *Anglo-American Cataloguing Rules,* 2d ed., 1988 revision (Chicago: American Library Association, 1988), xiii (hereafter cited as *AACR2R*).
2. Charles Martell, "War of AACR2: Victors or Victims," *Journal of Academic Librarianship* 7 (March 1981): 5.
3. American Library Association, Resources and Technical Services Division, Cataloging and Classification Section, Committee on Cataloging: Description and Access, Minutes, June 27–29, 1981, 12 (hereafter cited as CC:DA Minutes).
4. CC:DA Minutes, June 27–29, 1981, 12.
5. Joint Steering Committee for Revision of AACR, Minutes of the third meeting . . . 1 and 2 July 1981, 18.
6. Martell, "War of AACR2."
7. Janet Swan Hill, "Descriptions of Reproductions of Previously Existing Works: Another View," *Microform Review* 11 (Winter 1982): 14.
8. C. Sumner Spalding, "The Life and Death(?) of Corporate Authorship," *Library Resources & Technical Services* 24 (Summer 1980):195–208.
9. *Anglo-American Cataloging Rules,* North American Text (Chicago: American Library Association, 1967), 1.
10. *AACR2R,* 351.
11. Sanford Berman, "Cataloging for Public Libraries," in *The Nature and Future of the Catalog,* ed. Maurice J. Freedman and S. Michael Malinconico (Phoenix, Ariz.: Oryx Press, 1979), 226.
12. John Duke, "Authors and Names: Multiple Pseudonyms in AACR," *Cataloging and Classification Quarterly* 1 (Fall 1980): 78.
13. Duke, "Authors and Names," 88.
14. Bruce Ford, "New Attempts to Resolve Old Conflicts: Chapter 22 of AACR2," *Library Resources & Technical Services* 24 (Summer 1980): 214.
15. CC:DA Minutes, June 27–29, 1986, 7.
16. Ben R. Tucker, Memorandum to RI recipients, on pseudonyms (22.2C), March 15, 1988.
17. Frances Hinton, JSC Decisions made on September 1–2, 1982. Unpublished report to Nancy John, RTSD CCS CC:DA Chair, Oct. 25, 1982, 1.
18. CC:DA Minutes, Jan. 7–8, 1983, 10.
19. Ben R. Tucker, Letter to Nancy John, RTSD CCS CC:DA Chair, on microcomputer programs, Nov. 19, 1982.

20. Glenn Patton, Letter to Nancy John, RTSD CCS CC:DA Chair, on microcomputer software packages, Aug. 25, 1982.

21. American Library Association, Resources and Technical Services Division, Cataloging and Classification Section, Committee on Cataloging: Description and Access, *Guidelines for Using AACR2 Chapter 9 for Cataloging Microcomputer Software* (Chicago: American Library Association, 1984).

22. *Anglo-American Cataloguing Rules. Revised Chapter 9* (Chicago: American Library Association, 1987), iii.

23. Sue A. Dodd, "Changing AACR2 to Accommodate the Cataloging of Microcomputer Software," *Library Resources & Technical Services* 29 (1985): 55.

24. Dodd, "Changing AACR2."

25. American Library Association, Resources and Technical Services Division, Cataloging and Classification Section, Committee on Cataloging: Description and Access, Memorandum to Joint Steering Committee on revision of 9.0B1, Feb. 19, 1982.

26. Nurieh Mesavi, "An Evaluation of AACR2," *Library Resources & Technical Services* 30 (1986): 146.

The Continuous Revision Process

Richard P. Smiraglia

The calm with which the 1988 revision of AACR2 was greeted is evidence of the success of the process of continuous revision that was instituted following the introduction of AACR2 in 1978. Designed to prevent jarring changes in descriptive cataloging, the process has ensured the retention of pragmatic rules and the extension of principles derived from decades of study and international negotiation. This process, which continues even now, employs a complex of representative, deliberative bodies to assure a fair and rational approach to the evolution of descriptive cataloging. In this article an overview of the continuous revision process is presented, and three examples of how the process has worked are described.

The Revision Process

There are many participants in the process of code development and revision. In fact, there are several layers of participants, each with a slightly different mission.

The very top layer is the group known as the AACR Principals, consisting of the chief executive officer of each of the five original author bodies (American Library Association, Library Association, Canadian Library Association, British Library, and Library of Congress) plus the National Library of Canada. The group was given formal status in 1989 and has general managerial oversight of the other groups responsible for the maintenance of the code, including the timing of revised printings. These other groups are the Publishers, the AACR Revision Fund, and the Joint Steering Committee for Revision of AACR. The Publishers, or Copyright Holders, are the group responsible for the physical production and distribution of the code. Each of the parties to the agreement among the Publishers (who, by the way are the library associations, not their respective publishing enterprises) also appoints a trustee of the AACR Revision Fund. This fund is derived from a portion of the royalties from the sale of the code. The trustees advise on the fund's investment and expenditure, which at present must be for "travel and subsistence expenses of the members of the Joint Steering Committee."[1]

A representative of each of the author institutions is appointed to serve as a member of the Joint Steering Committee (JSC, officially the Joint Steering Committee for Revision of AACR), which has responsibility for the code's provisions. The members of JSC are:

1. The American Library Association, whose representative is advised by the Committee on Cataloging: Description and Access (CC:DA, a committee of the Cataloging and Classification Section of the Association for Library Collections & Technical Services, formerly the Resources and Technical Services Division);
2. The Library of Congress;
3. The British Library;
4. The Library Association (the British Library and the Library Association often act in unison under the joint guise of the LABL Committee);
5. The Canadian Committee on Cataloguing, representing diverse Canadian interests and including representatives of both the Canadian Library Association and the National Library of Canada; and,
6. The Australian Committee on Cataloguing, representing similarly diverse groups and including representatives of both the Australian Library and Information Association and the National Library of Australia.

The JSC that was responsible for the 1988 revision was known as 2JSCAACR, because it was the JSC formed after publication of AACR2. The editors, Michael Gorman and Paul W. Winkler, were voting members of 2JSCAACR. Following the publication of the 1988 revision, the JSC was reconstituted as 3JSCAACR. At present there is no editor functioning as a member of 3JSCAACR.

The Canadians and Australians have developed supra-institutional bodies, national committees on cataloging, to advise their JSC representatives. The newest participant is the Australian Committee on Cataloguing (ACOC), which joined the JSC only after the 1978 publication of AACR2, and which is not currently a party to the AACR Principals agreement. The chair of the JSC is elected from among the members.

The JSC has a complex charge, which basically boils down to a few major points:

1. to keep under review the need for amendment and revision, and any abridgment or translation;
2. to prepare for publication any necessary amendments to and revisions of AACR2 (hence the 1982, 1983, and 1985 revision packets);
3. to ensure the integrity of the publication; and,
4. to assess the use and sale of the code, and to advise its users.[2]

In the United States, CC:DA has the following responsibilities:

1. making a continuing assessment of the state of the art and suggesting the direction of change in the field of descriptive cataloging;
2. instructing the ALA representative to the JSC regarding the official ALA position and suggesting suitable bases for negotiation;
3. developing ALA positions on international standards for descriptive cataloging; and,
4. encouraging the United States library and information service community to express opinions on these matters.[3]

CC:DA's membership is complex. Eight voting members and a chair (who traditionally votes only to break a tie) are appointed by the Cataloging and Classification Section. Nonvoting representatives and liaisons fall into three groups. First, the ALA representative to the JSC, and representatives from the Library of Congress, OCLC Online Computer Library Center, and the Research Libraries Group are specifically stipulated in the committee's charter. Second, a group of representatives of about twenty ALA units also serve as nonvoting members of the committee. These groups, such as the representative of the Public Library Association, serve to give a voice in the development of the code to all parts of ALA. Finally, representatives of sixteen non-ALA units also serve as nonvoting members of the committee. These units, such as the Medical Library Association, the Music Library Association, the Society of American Archivists, and the Art Libraries Society of North America all are groups that can be defined as national in scope and specialist in orientation, and each group has its own deliberative body with responsibility for cataloging. The inclusion of such special user groups helps ensure broad-based support for the code and is considered essential to accomplish the committee's charge, which is to speak for the entire United States library community in matters of descriptive cataloging.

That this structure is deliberately representative can be discerned in the annual reports of the ALA Cataloging and Classification Section (CCS) Executive Committee through the 1970s. In 1970, as the old Descriptive Cataloging Committee (DCC) met with its Anglo-American partners to discuss coordination of changes in AACR, it was noted that specialist expertise and access to the Library of Congress were particular problems, as was the increasing necessity to internationalize descriptive cataloging. CCS charged its Policy and Research Committee to recommend a new structure to help alleviate these problems.[4] By 1973 the internationalization of the code had become a reality with the appearance of the *International Standard Bibliographic Description (Monographs)* (ISBD (M)).

CCS had considered (and rejected) the notion of a "national cataloging committee with an almost permanent membership of acknowledged 'experts.' " ALA at the highest levels had been unwilling to place the problems of long-term international cooperation in a higher priority position than its association-wide commitment to the concept that "each member's opinion is as valuable as another's and should find scope to be heard."[5] The interim problem of revising AACR was resolved by appointing the Catalog Code Revision Committee (CCRC) at the ALA Resources and Technical Services Division divisional level, and making DCC a resource unit to advise it.

By 1977, CCS had recognized "increasing interest in matters of cataloging and classification within other divisions of ALA, including sections of other divisions . . . although the question of how these mutual interests are best pursued . . . is a complex one."[6] A year later, CCS received the blessing of the RTSD Board of Directors when it returned to CCS the responsibility for care of the code (by now AACR2 was at press) and for nominating ALA's representative to the new JSC.

CCS also had acknowledged "that catalogers specializing in area materials feel the need for an opportunity to discuss and seek solutions to their area-oriented problems."[7] Thus the new committee, CC:DA, which met first in Dallas in 1979, was structured like CCRC, with "a strong commitment to provide the broadest possible input."[8]

These, then, are the participants in the revision process. Each has a separate mission, but collectively all have a common goal, which is the process that results in the continuous monitoring of the Anglo-American provisions.

This process is actually rather simple if somewhat circuitous, incorporating repeated consultations between and among layers in order to produce consensus on any issue. A proposal may be generated at any level, by any person or body. The JSC is the body that makes the definitive decisions about the rules themselves. To get on its agenda it is best for a proposal to come from one of the member bodies. For example, a letter from a practicing cataloger addressed to the JSC will usually be referred to the various national bodies for comment. With only rare exceptions, proposals forwarded to the JSC by one of the member bodies will likewise be referred to all the other parties for comment. Because the JSC members all act as representatives to some extent, they will in turn consult their various constituencies. In the United States, a letter to CC:DA will be distributed to all the members, voting and nonvoting. Most proposals, whether generated by a CC:DA member or received from outside, usually are referred to a task force for detailed study and comment, a process that normally lasts six months but can occasionally take longer. Following the task force's report, CC:DA must vote whether to pursue the proposal. Before the voting members act, they probably will want the advice of a straw poll of the nonvoting members. Often, when CC:DA has voted to pursue a proposed revision, another task force will be appointed to draft the formal proposal.

Proposals with sufficient merit to survive scrutiny by the national committees and national libraries will get on the JSC's formal agenda. The JSC usually operates by consensus, which is to say that they are extremely reluctant to accept any proposal so long as any member still objects. However, if and when the members have decided in the affirmative, a project is assigned to an editor for a draft.[9] When a draft has been produced, the whole process starts all over again as the draft is circulated to all of the national groups and their advisory bodies for comment. This back-and-forth process continues until no one has anything left to say about the proposal. This process often lasts three to five years, depending on the degree of controversy (or confusion) surrounding any given proposal.

Continuous Revision: The Rationale

Why continuous revision? Why not just issue a new code every twenty years? Why deliberative, representative bodies rather than permanent authors with autocratic independence? There are several answers to these questions.

First, the process is deliberative because the Anglo-American rules represent a consensus on the current operational paradigm in descriptive cataloging. Consequently, it is necessary that any proposed change be given the broadest possible exposure so as to ensure the broadest possible contribution to discussions surrounding it.

Second, the process is deliberately slow paced to avoid surprises in the form of unexpected radical (or even minor but expensive) changes. As Peter Lewis pointed out, "in cataloging, all changes cost money."[10] But as he also noted:

> Failure to keep cataloging practice in line with changes in the characteristics in the documents in our libraries, and with the expectations and needs of document users in those libraries, leads to increasing inefficiencies; [thus] the longer the changes are deferred, the more they cost [and, therefore,] the proper method is to carry out revisions promptly.[11]

Third, the process is democratic, or at least representative. This, too, was deliberate. At the time of the 1978 publication of AACR, Lewis, who had chaired the JSC responsible for its authorship, noted the introduction of "an element of democratic approval, as well as international harmony."[12] Politically this might be the most important aspect of the revision process, for this is the means employed to ensure the broadest possible support for the resulting code, by allowing everyone a voice in its development and therefore a vested interest in the continued success of the joint venture.

This was behind the rationale for the representative structure of CC:DA. Controversies such as those over the description of microform reproductions, entry under pseudonyms, and the physical description of computer files have not deterred the committee from its goal of gathering the broadest possible advice to achieve the broadest possible consent.

How to Influence Revision of the Rules

As noted above, the committee, editorial, and advisory structure, and the revision process, are designed to allow broad participation in the development of the code. Every librarian has a voice in rule revision and can influence the process. Also, perhaps more importantly, every librarian has a responsibility to the profession and to the reading public to take part in the revision of the rules. To illustrate, three stories from the annals of rule revision follow, in order to describe three particular approaches to rule revision. Two of these approaches were successful on their own; the third would not have succeeded without the assistance of the Australians.

Music Revisions

The first story is about music. Music librarians had a lot to be angry about when they saw the final edition of AACR in 1978.[13] There is a long tradition in music cataloging, going back to the origins of the Music Library Association in the 1930s and to the production during the 1940s and 1950s of a draft code for cataloging printed and recorded music. Many of the provisions set out in that draft code had been incorporated since the 1949 red and green books into the standard cataloging codes. But somehow, when AACR was produced, the new rules raised more questions than they answered. There were three major categories into which these problems fell. First, there were many problems with the descriptive provisions in chapters 5 and 6. To some extent these problems arose from the separation of rules that had been necessary to develop the integrated approach to Part I of the code. Thus, in chapter 5 we were told to record the title proper as instructed in chapter 1, but nowhere were we told how to handle all of the various words and phrases that might appear on printed music, let alone which of these would constitute the title proper.

A second set of problems was associated with the rules for choice of entry for sound recordings. This was probably a more serious problem, and definitely a more contentious problem, if to some extent confounded with the issue of main entry. Chapter 21 had now incorporated rules allowing entry of some sound recordings under performers' names. This represented a major innovation because it forced catalogers to approach recordings discographically; that is, recordings were now to be considered as "performances" and entered under the heading for the performer. However, the rule as written in the 1978 code was simply inadequate, and it was clear that revision would be required. Finally, the rules for constructing music uniform titles had two problems. One was that the rules were in a very strange order, such that any attempt to construct a uniform title required a great deal of page turning and flip-flopping to get through the maze successfully. Second, the attempt to conflate British and North American practices had resulted in a rule that was practically unworkable, and it certainly led to results that were to the liking of almost no one. Rule 5.7A instructed the use of the original title of a musical work in the language in which it was formulated. This provision was based on the North American practice in AACR of using the title of the first edition. However, rule 5.7A also instructed the preference of a later title in the same language that was better known. This was derived from the British approach in AACR of employing the best-known title of a musical work. The outcome of combining these provisions was:

1. Every uniform title had to be formulated from scratch (that is, uniform titles established under earlier codes could not be used), because the standard approach, which had been to use the title proper on any item that was a first edition and to find a description of the first edition for any other work, no longer was valid.
2. It was necessary to guess the language of the composer at the time the piece was written (for example, were Bach's works with Latin texts written in German or Latin?).
3. It was necessary to know the original title, which usually could be determined only through extensive searching in reference sources.
4. If it turned out that the work had a better known title in the same language, it was to be preferred. The problem with this was with works that are better known to English-speakers by English titles. The classic examples are Tchaikovsky's works, now entered under their Russian titles, thus *Sleeping Beauty* has become *Spiaschaiîa krasaviîsa*.

It was clear to the music cataloging community that revisions would be needed immediately. The sound recording issue was the first to be taken up by the Music Library Association (MLA). MLA joined forces with the Association for Recorded Sound Collections (ARSC), and also with the British, Canadian, and Australian branches of the International Association of Music Libraries. Together the representatives of these organizations developed a hierarchical approach whereby:

1. recordings with collective titles were treated as performances;
2. recordings without collective titles were treated as compositions if they were in the Western art or classical tradition; and,
3. recordings without collective titles that were not in the Western art tradition were treated as performances.

Subsequent research indicated that this was a useful approach, because recordings tend to present themselves in these ways. MLA and ARSC made a proposal along these lines to CC:DA, and music representatives in Britain, Canada, and Australia were encouraged to coach their own JSC representatives to agree with the proposal when it came forward from CC:DA. This particular revision took a rather long time to wend its way through the process, because writing the rule was not easy and many drafts were expended on it, but by the time LC implemented AACR in 1981, the revision was sufficiently documented that LC was able to incorporate it into a rule interpretation for interim use until the first revision packet appeared in 1982.

Once this problem was more or less settled, MLA set about carefully examining AACR for other music problems. This led to successive drafts (within MLA) of a lengthy document detailing each problem that had been encountered in cataloging or user service with the new rules. Hearings were held at successive MLA meetings until a consensus was achieved on all points (all, that is, but the uniform title problem). The resulting document had two sections. First were problems that demanded immediate solution. CC:DA demanded and got evidence of each problem in the form of title page surrogates and potentially problematic cataloging. Eventually each of these was sent forward to the JSC by CC:DA, and most were incorporated into the 1983 revision packet.

However, music catalogers remained at loggerheads about the uniform title problems. On the one hand, the problems with the order of the rules were not difficult, but it was clear that revision would necessitate reprinting the whole of chapter 25. On the other hand, the problem with the language of the uniform title was and still is a major problem, but no consensus had been reached about how the rule could or should be changed. Thus, the problems were documented and referred to CC:DA for information, but no revision was requested. Once it became clear that there would be a new edition of the code, CC:DA requested MLA to resubmit the proposal for the reordering of the rules in chapter 25, and that revision is part of the 1988 revision. The other problem remains unresolved, and probably will continue to do so, until such time as the music library community comes to some reasonable conclusion about potential solutions. So, in this first case, concerted action by a group of specialists employing their skills and expertise to identify both problems and potential solutions got the attention of the revision process and yielded revisions that are for the most part sensible and workable.

Places of Publication

The second story has to do with the rule for transcription of places of publication. In AACR, according to rule 138B, for a work that "gives indication of being published in several places by one publisher ... [it] is generally described ... [by] the first named place ... and the corresponding publisher."[14] The rule then went on to say to prefer some other place or publisher that is clearly distinguishable as the principal place or publisher. Finally, if a city in the country of the cataloging agency is given in a secondary position, it was to be included in addition to the foreign imprint. This provision was well known for decades (it can be found in rule 3:10A in the 1949 rules), and was applied automatically by experienced catalogers.[15]

Arlene G. Taylor, an experienced cataloger, cataloging scholar, former member of CC:DA, and, in 1983, assistant professor of cataloging at the University of Chicago's Graduate Library School, had given a descriptive cataloging assignment, in response to which her students (who of course had no experience) had followed the current rule as written in AACR2, which said to give the first named place and any subsequently named place in the country of the cataloging agency. The effect was to give both places of publication, which to an experienced cataloger, looked incorrect.

An examination of a portion of the University of Chicago's Regenstein Library backlog yielded several books with more than one United States city on their title pages. The LC copy for these books was located in OCLC and, as one might have expected, all were described by giving only the first named place. Thus, although the wording of AACR2 said one thing, it was clear that nobody had been expecting to encounter a change in that rule from AACR, and consequently no catalogers had noticed that they were not following the rule as written.

A letter, accompanied by copies of the title pages of the backlogged books and the accompanying LC cataloging, was sent to CC:DA. The members were dumbfounded—nobody had noticed the changed rule—but quickly agreed to propose a revision, which was forwarded to the JSC and eventually incorporated into the 1988 revision.

The lesson is that changes sometimes creep into rules in the editorial process. It can be useful to gather evidence of misapplication of a rule, including corresponding rules in preceding codes, to see whether an apparent change was deliberate. Then, a letter to CC:DA, providing evidence of the problem and proposing a solution, can be an appropriate spur to rule revision.

Pseudonyms and Petitions

The third and final revision story has to do with the rule on choice of name and, in particular, with the entry of people who use pseudonyms. This, too, is a brief story, and the point of it is that in order to succeed at rule revision it is important to follow the procedural rules.

Helen Schmierer, as ALA's representative to the JSC, received a letter suggesting several revision proposals, among them the idea that works published under pseudonyms should be entered under those pseudonyms rather than under the real name of the author. Her response was to submit the letter to CC:DA for its consideration. CC:DA was very busy at this time wrapping up the final texts of the revisions that would go into the 1988 publication. The author of this letter came to a meeting of CC:DA and grew very angry that the committee did not get to the new proposals.

At any rate, about a year earlier the Australian Committee on Cataloguing had proposed a similar approach to pseudonyms. The Library of Congress was sympathetic to this proposal (which is described elsewhere in this volume in more detail),[16] both from its own experience and because of requests it had received from the Public Library Association. CC:DA appointed a task force, which struggled with the problem and ultimately recommended a revision. The revision sets up a hierarchy of pseudonyms, in which works by authors using several pseudonyms can be entered under the pseudonyms, all of which are linked using "see also" references. So the revision was successful, largely because it came at a time when several interests converged and because the evidence was clear that a revision was necessary.

But the story doesn't end here; several harassing letters and a petition drive later the original author is still asking CC:DA to review the original proposals. This person, and the hundreds who've signed the petitions, remain unaware that the issues proposed have been discussed, that CC:DA has taken action on those with which it agrees, and that for all intents and purposes the subject is closed.

So, the moral of this story is: pay attention to the work of the various committees involved in rule revision, insofar as it is possible work within the system, and present rational arguments backed up with clear evidence.

Conclusion

This article began by mentioning the quiet success of the continuous revision process. As Peter Lewis noted, the process was implemented following the publication of AACR2 to prevent the sudden introduction of radically different provisions with their attendant cost implications. The result has been a monumental contribution to bibliographic control. The success of the process is evidenced in the calm with which the revised rules were anticipated on all fronts.

The process has worked, not just adequately but extraordinarily well for all its cumbersome layers and procedures. Collectively the author bodies have been sensitive to new and evolving technologies (as evidenced by the new provisions for digital audio discs and microcomputer software). They have retained the pragmatic structure of the code and reinforced its principles through consistent application (as evidenced by extension of provisions such as parallelism and the use of area 3). And, they have accomplished all of this while simultaneously resisting efforts to co-opt their time with proposals of purely parochial interest (such as repeated proposals to abandon the ISBD framework at the cost of international cooperation).

As the term "continuous revision" implies, the process goes on. Even now, CC:DA is debating new proposals for revision to the code, and this is an exciting time for code revisers. Areas demanding attention include the profession's continued embrace of automated systems, the emerging growth in authority control acknowledging the distinction between items and works, attention recently focused on the concept of the catalog as a relational database, and the addition of entirely new user groups to the cataloging family (for example, archivists, who because of the introduction of the MARC AMC format have begun to use AACR2 to formulate archival descriptions). All of these offer exciting opportunities for those willing to participate in this challenging process.

Finally, some advice for those who would succeed at rule revision:

1. First, know the system and utilize it to its fullest extent. Be aware that ideas must pass the scrutiny of numerous deliberative bodies because, if they are accepted, they will represent an international consensus.
2. Any individual can contribute either by working through any of the thirty or so special bodies that have representation on CC:DA, or by making a proposal either alone or with a colleague.
3. Arguments should be presented in simple language and should suggest equitable solutions. Tangible evidence that a problem exists should accompany any proposal. This can be in the form of photocopies of items, the cataloging of them that needs to change, and an illustration of how the changed cataloging would look.
4. Correspondence should be directed to the current chair of CC:DA, for the backing of the ALA makes a powerful statement to the JSC and its other national constituents.

Notes

1. Memorandum, Marion Reid, President, RTSD, to Thomas F. Galvin, June 30, 1987, "Comments on Agreements Related to the Anglo-American Cataloguing Rules," 5–6.
2. Memorandum, Helen F. Schmierer to RTSD Directors, Jan. 1987, "Agreements Related to the Anglo-American Cataloguing Rules," [7–8].

3. *ALA Handbook of Organization, 1987/1988* (Chicago: American Library Association, 1987), 142.
4. Koch, Esther D. "Cataloging and Classification Section Report," *Library Resources & Technical Services* 14 (Fall 1970): 599.
5. Hagler, Ronald, " Cataloging and Classification Section Report," *Library Resources & Technical Services* 15 (Fall 1973): 444.
6. Moore, Jane Ross, "Cataloging and Classification Section Report," *Library Resources & Technical Services* 21 (Winter 1977): 86.
7. Tate, Elizabeth L., "Cataloging and Classification Section Report," *Library Resources & Technical Services* 23 (Winter 1979): 80.
8. Nilson, Julie, "Cataloging and Classification Section," *Library Resources & Technical Services* 25 (Jan./March 1981): 114.
9. The editors usually volunteer for these assignments, the JSC being a pretty good-natured group.
10. Lewis, Peter, "The Politics of Catalog Code Revision and Future Considerations," in *The Making of a Code,* ed. Doris Hargrett Clack (Chicago: American Library Association, 1980), 5.
11. Lewis, "Politics of Catalog Code Revision," 5.
12. Lewis, "Politics of Catalog Code Revision," 15.
13. For a brief history see "Descriptive Cataloging," in Richard P. Smiraglia, *Music Cataloging: The Bibliographic Control of Printed and Recorded Music in Libraries* (Englewood, Colo.: Libraries Unlimited, 1990), 1–6.
14. *Anglo-American Cataloging Rules,* North American text (Chicago: American Library Association, 1967), 200.
15. Library of Congress, Descriptive Cataloging Division. *Rules for Descriptive Cataloging in the Library of Congress* (Washington: Library of Congress, 1949), 16.
16. See Olivia M. A. Madison, "A Summary of Changes in AACR2 Revised," 5–7; and, Elaine N. Hall, "The Third 'A' on JSCAACR," 32–33, in this volume.

The Third "A" on JSCAACR

Elaine N. Hall

Australia Gains Entry

The minutes of the meeting of the Joint Steering Committee for Revision of AACR (JSCAACR, or JSC) held in Tallahassee on March 15–16, 1979, include under item 7, Purpose of Meeting, a somewhat enigmatic subsection 7.6: "The question was raised whether there had been any formal request for Australian representation on JSC. It was AGREED to defer this matter pending further information" (p. 2).

In fact, in a letter dated February 28, 1979, the executive director of the Library Association of Australia (LAA) had written on behalf of the Association's Committee on International Cataloguing to Dorothy Anderson, director of the IFLA International Office for UBC, asking her to convey to the members of JSC a formal request for Australian membership of the JSC. The letter noted that:

> The LAA has for some time been contributing to cataloguing code revision and to the review of draft standards documents sent from overseas. For instance, the Australian Law Librarians' Group Study Group on Descriptive Cataloguing compiled recommendations on Anglo-American cataloguing rules 20–26; these were submitted in 1971 before the commencement of work on AACR2 was announced. Latterly, the Committee on International Cataloguing of the LAA Cataloguers Section has submitted comments on several draft documents issued by the International Office for UBC. However, it is felt that it is not really satisfactory only to contribute

when one wishes changes to be made. It would be more meaningful to be fully aware of which rules were under scrutiny, to have a stronger voice to support our opinions, and to be able to comment on the opinions of others.

At the second meeting of the JSC held in Vancouver in June 1980, Peter Lewis reported from the chair on the receipt of that letter. The minutes of that meeting note that in discussion members expressed the opinion that a precedent might be created and that it would be costly to admit the Library Association of Australia to membership. Nonetheless the minutes went on to record:

> 26.3.4 It was AGREED that in view of Australia's close relationship with the other English speaking countries and its national library's membership of ABACUS it should be admitted to membership of JSC.

> 26.3.5 It was AGREED to recommend to the Trustees of the Common Revision Fund that an invitation should be extended to Australia, in the form of a single representative of both the Library Association of Australia and the National Library of Australia, to become a member of JSC in recognition of the exceptionally close relationships between Australian practitioners and the Anglo-American communities; and that an increased participation in JSC's work from this quarter was a legitimate use of funds (p. 3).

Members attending that meeting were advised to consult with their constituencies to obtain their approval for this invitation to be issued; this approval was obtained as a special case and with no implication that any other requests for membership in JSC would be welcomed. Frances Hinton, as chairperson of JSC, conveyed this information to the Trustees of the Common Revision Fund in a memo of July 31, 1980. In that memo she also made reference to the fact that apparently the National Library of Australia had sent a similar request two years earlier to the RTSD office of the American Library Association, but that the request appears not to have been acted upon.

Consequent on the Trustees endorsing this recommendation, on January 31, 1981, Frances Hinton wrote to the Library Association of Australia, inviting Australia to select a member to represent the interests of all segments of the Australian library community on the Joint Steering Committee.

The Trustees of the Common Revision Fund had determined that the fund could provide up to U.S. $1,600 for the annual expenses of a member from

Australia, with the hope that the sponsoring bodies in Australia would be willing to supplement this amount as necessary. Indeed, from the third through to the ninth meeting, the National Library of Australia and the Library Association of Australia shared the additional expenses of sending the Australian representative.

The invitation to send one member representing both the National Library and the Library Association suited Australia very well and placed the Australian representation on the same basis as the Canadian.

Jan Fullerton, then principal librarian (cataloguing) at the National Library of Australia, was selected to be the first Australian representative and attended the third meeting of the JSC held in San Francisco in July 1981.

Contrary to the concerns expressed by members at the second meeting, JSC was not besieged with requests for JSC membership; extending the membership to Australian representation might therefore be interpreted as giving credence to the proposition that this was a logical rounding-out and -off step for JSC.

This simple retelling of the process of Australia achieving membership of JSC does not do justice to the work of a number of Australian librarians over several years. They were confident that Australia could make a worthwhile contribution to the development of cataloging standards, and they worked hard on laying the groundwork to get Australia recognized; the fact that the process described above appears to have flowed so smoothly is a credit to their efforts. However I have resisted the temptation to name names because of the real danger of offending through inadvertent omission.

ACOC Is Born

While these transactions had been taking place at the international level, there had been a welter of activity in Australia. Firstly, the National Library had been heavily involved in preparations leading up to implementation of AACR2 in January 1981. Secondly, preparations had been under way for the first meeting of the Australian Committee on Cataloguing in May 1981.

The Australian Committee on Cataloguing was established as a Working Party of the Australian Advisory Council on Bibliographical Services (AACOBS), being a joint AACOBS/Library Association of Australia/National Library of Australia committee; it initially had eight members, but with a third National Library representative added subsequently it brought the representation to three per body.

AACOBS was the driving force behind the formation of the committee; their prime concern at that time was the effect that international bibliographic standards were having on Australian institutions and the desirability of consultation before changes were made to these standards. In particular at this time, the alarmist reporting that had appeared in a range of international professional journals, relating to the cost and impact on catalogs of introducing AACR2, had certainly succeeded in alarming AACOBS and provoked them into action. They determined to set up a committee to monitor, attempt to influence, and report on international cataloging issues. And, while recognizing the contribution that representatives from the National Library and the LAA would make, they were particularly concerned to have members on the committee who would add to their technical judgment a recognition of the implication of rule changes from the point of view of efficient library management and the realities of the library environment.

It is worth expanding further on this point because, while trusting that the Australian representation on JSC has made a worthwhile contribution to the direction of AACR2 rule revision, that same Australian membership has at home made a notable contribution to an improved perception of catalogers and cataloging.

It is always dangerous to generalize. However, Australian catalogers— among whom there have been many fine professionals, dedicated practitioners, and fine teachers—have not generally moved up in organizations to senior management and chief executive positions in as great numbers as librarians from the "reader services" side of librarianship. Librarians fully conversant and up to date with cataloging practices and developments have not usually been at the forefront of setting the strategic direction and consequent resource allocation in libraries. It had reached the point towards the end of the 1970s where the library managers seemed to have lost touch with what was going on in the world of cataloging. While understandably not interested in the minutiae of cataloging, in letting go at that level they had inadvertently lost communication and understanding at the level where they in fact needed it. But in all cases where there is a breakdown in communication it is only appropriate that "blame" be apportioned to both sides. And it is to the credit of AACOBS that they took the initiative in setting up a committee that—for a wealth of reasons—has been effective. I believe that ACOC, whose focus of activity has been briefing the Australian representative to JSC and reporting on the work of that committee, has earned the respect of library managers. It has also demonstrated that, in attending to developments on the technical side of cataloging, it is possible to bear in mind the very practical realities of the impact of bibliographic standards.

And the hope is that an Australian chief librarian will never again be moved to declare that "cataloguing is too important to be left to the cataloguers," paraphrasing the variously attributed and quoted statement that "war is too important to be left to the generals."[1]

ACOC in Action

Australia adopted a deliberately low-key approach in its early contribution to the work of JSC. Before the third JSC meeting, in fact, the Australian Committee on Cataloguing was not operational for long enough to be organized into its role of discussing JSC issues and briefing the Australian representative.

It was not easy breaking into the JSC process. JSC has since taken some important steps to improve the management of the process of getting changes through the approval mechanism. They should assist newcomers to graduate with fewer bruises and traumas than we in ACOC sustained in the process of getting on top of the system. The overriding memory from ACOC meetings is the struggle to conquer the paper mountain and to maintain a filing system that would withstand dealing with agenda items out of sequence, while remaining coolly dextrous with all the rules, their interrelationships, and their pedigree. As time went on it became a serious game of mental gymnastics just to stay on top of the definitive version of the rules. The real test for full membership of ACOC came when one was faced on arrival in Canberra with a newly received bundle of papers, and this was after those who had to fly in to the capital—fog permitting—had honed their nonchalance skills at the airport check-in, tripping on to the plane with just that theoretical 10kg only carry-on luggage. How could one trust such valuable cargo to the hold! How could one forego the opportunity to gain another inspiration to squash or praise a revision proposal in that brief snatch of extra study time! And what finer imprint could one's personal effects have than to be permanently pressed by AACR2 rule revisions! But the meetings brought with them in full measure that facility for building up a wonderful camaraderie that is one of the many rewards of professional involvement.

From preparing and circulating written responses only on those documents where a contrary or supplementary view was the result of discussion at the ACOC meeting, ACOC adopted a deliberate policy to prepare an Australian response on every paper for discussion at the JSC meetings; this took effect from the sixth JSC meeting. In a number of cases the response was an endorsement of the position taken in the original document or in one of its often numerous subsequent manifestations. However, ACOC considered it important to give a clear message that the Committee had addressed and developed a position on every issue.

Unlike a number of other JSC members, ACOC did not, of course, have a carryover agenda from meetings before the publication of AACR2. We were also exhorted to remain conscious of the mood of JSC that was reported to us as conservative and with the ethos of minimum change. Although the first Australian paper proposing a rule revision change did not appear on a JSC agenda until its seventh meeting in 1985, ACOC had received requests from Australian librarians from the start to put forward proposals for revision. For example, dissatisfaction with rule 24.18 was drawn to the attention of ACOC members at its first meeting in May 1981. However, after the initial knee-jerk reaction, a combination of familiarity breeding content (instead of contempt) and the difficulty of seeing how the rule could be effectively improved, led to the eventual lapse of the move for change to this rule.

A number of other early representations for rule change were not formally proposed because, while ACOC essentially agreed with the arguments for change, satisfactory solutions were not perceived. Two of these early representations eventually were catered for with revisions arising from other papers; these were the revision of the GMD "machine-readable data file," and the change to rule 23.4G, "Places in cities."

Paper 2JSC/Aus/1 received rather peremptory treatment at its first airing at the seventh meeting of JSC in Chicago in August of 1985. At least the minutes just recorded: "It was agreed to defer this item until 1986 until further consultation on the probable consequences of its implementation has taken place" (p. 18).

The paper referred to was a proposal to change the then-rule 22.2C, "Pseudonyms." My notes from that meeting record that concern was expressed about the rule in its proposed revised form also being applied to writers who used pseudonyms for political reasons, but whose works should be brought together for research purposes.

There was nothing more that Australia could do however but wait until the Toronto meeting of JSC in March 1986. The minutes record a good resolution from Australia's point of view:

> 152.10.2 After much discussion, JSC decided that the problem related only to contemporary original English-language fiction. Michael will rewrite 22.2C for circulation incorporating the above and advising the use of a predominant name if it is evident without research; otherwise, the name on the title page is to be given (p. 7).

Obviously I was more emotionally involved, and my report on that meeting (written up, I remember very clearly, in San Francisco while overnighting on the way back to Australia) for circulation to ACOC members gave more details of the discussion. I noted that the proposal, while receiving widespread popular support, was considered a real attack on the principle of Anglo-American cataloging and, if adopted, a representation of a complete shift in the rules. Particular concern was expressed about the political and strategic problems and about the validity of the proposal for both pre-twentieth century and non-Western authors.

The 1988 revision is witness to the ultimate acceptance of the rule revision proposal with a substantially rewritten rule 22.2B, "Pseudonyms," incorporating the newly identified concept of "separate bibliographic identities." One can only say that when Australia did put forward a rule revision proposal it was not shy in what it attempted.

However, standing back now, the most important aspect of this rule revision was that it addressed an access issue, not a technical issue. Furthermore, it did not arise out of an access issue relating to esoteric research material; it originated from public librarians—specifically the public librarians of Western Australia—who were concerned with being able to follow the international standard, but who were sufficiently worried about what the users of that catalog would make of the product, that they made a case for change.[2] It is a lesson that I think is worth going back to; the purpose of the catalog is to provide access to recorded information. That recorded information covers the whole gamut of what might variously be called information, knowledge, entertainment, education, recreation, and culture. But the role of the catalog is to provide access to it all, and if a rule inhibits access for public library users to their bread-and-butter novels whose authors regularly engage in pseudonymous shifts, then the issue is as worthy of our concern as any other.

By way of contrast, the second Australian proposal was an agenda item at that same meeting in 1985 and was received as if it were a model of common sense and accepted with only minor changes. As a result there is a new rule 26.5 in the 1988 revision entitled "References to Added Entries for Series and Serials." Two more contrasting receptions for the first two rule revision proposals from a JSC participant would be difficult to imagine.

Australia's third foray into initiating rule revision foundered at its first hearing, at the eighth meeting in March 1986. The proposal related to headings for Vietnamese names entered in direct order, requesting that a comma not be used after the initial element. The argument against changing the rule was that in this case the comma does not indicate inversion, rather the setting off of main elements. Therefore, although aesthetically the result may not be pleasing, it is not inherently incorrect. The point also was made and accepted at the meeting that the rule could not be changed for names relating to one language alone when the principles being advanced in the proposed revision applied equally to other languages such as Hungarian and Chinese. Australia did not feel competent to attack the issue in the scope it was conceded was necessary, especially taking into consideration the fast approaching deadline for agreement on changes for the 1988 revision. The fact that some automated filing systems could also require what would presumably be rather complex readjustment, should such a proposal be agreed to, added another twist and cautionary element.

The fourth, fifth, and sixth Australian proposals introduced onto the agenda for the ninth meeting of JSC in London in October 1986 all had relatively smooth passage through into the 1988 revision. They introduced what were obviously agreed to be worthwhile improvements into 12.7B1, the frequency note for serials; 21.3B, relating to changes in persons or bodies responsible for serials; and, 1.1E5, the transcribing of other title information.

Australia Achieves Joint Author Status

Parallel with the attention being given to the details of rule revision, ACOC had given considerable thought to its status with respect to JSC. This culminated in the ACOC chairperson writing in December 1985 to the five author bodies of the 1978 edition of the *Anglo-American Cataloguing Rules*. The purpose of the letter was to seek approval for Australia, under the name of the Australian Committee on Cataloguing, to become a full participant in the work of cataloging rule revision through being identified as a joint author of the *Anglo-American Cataloguing Rules*. Attention was drawn to ACOC's belief that participation in the rule revision process carried a significant responsibility; Australia was anxious to be formally identified with that challenge and indeed had already demonstrated its capacity to meet that responsibility.

Australia was very conscious of the political nature of this request, but was encouraged by the letters received early in 1986, for example from the deputy librarian of Congress. Understandably, however, the application required high-level consultation, and the IFLA Conference in Tokyo in August 1986 fortuitously provided an early forum for that to take place. We were very pleased to receive a letter dated December 17, 1986, from Thomas

Galvin, executive director of the American Library Association, who had been charged by the group of the representatives of the five organizations to convey to us the relevant outcome of the Tokyo discussions. The letter contained the following paragraph:

> I am pleased to report that it was unanimously agreed that the intellectual contribution of the Australian Committee on Cataloguing through its participation since 1981 in the work of the Joint Steering Committee should be recognized in the author statement of the forthcoming Consolidated Edition. Those present were also unanimous in supporting full Australian participation in the continuing work of the Joint Steering Committee (including the right to vote in that Committee) with funding to be provided on the same basis as to other JSC representatives. Ownership of copyright would, however, remain unchanged, as would any arrangements about market sharing.

It would be difficult to exaggerate to the Australian Committee on Cataloguing the significance of this achievement.

The 1988 Revision in Australia

If the truth be told, the actual publication of the 1988 revision was almost an anticlimax in Australia. The fact that it was a cause of not very particular concern, though, should really be considered the achievement of its (even if not explicitly stated) objective. Not that catalogers were not pleased to acquire a brand new copy of one of their standard working tools, with all the revisions incorporated into the one volume. (Many would also have liked to see the Library of Congress rule interpretations incorporated into the one volume, but that is the subject for another chapter in another book!)

However, the revisions had been so well heralded through the revision packages, through National Library of Australia announcements, Australian Bibliographic Network cataloging standards, and Library of Congress rule interpretations that the transition to formally cataloging according to AACR2 1988 revision was taken by catalogers in their stride. The changes were generally perceived as progressive and the overall result as a better code. It is also reasonable to conclude that one of the reasons why Australian catalogers did accept the revised version so readily was that we were known to have been involved in the revision process, so that the previous bogy of having unheralded changes imposed could not be wheeled out.

Beyond the 1988 Revision

Before the tenth meeting of the Joint Steering Committee in April 1989 the Australian Committee on Cataloguing took the opportunity provided by the Library Association/British Library paper on future priorities for the JSC to contemplate the future of the JSC and AACR2. ACOC was firmly of the view that there must be a mechanism for the revision of AACR2—a standard that does not allow for such a process in this changing, developing world would progressively become useless. It seems appropriate to me now to draw an analogy between AACR2 and a heavily used complex piece of sophisticated machinery. Such a piece of equipment needs regular maintenance, a complete check-up from time to time, the addition of new functions, and the rationalization of processes. But the machine remains essentially the same, in the same way that AACR2 1988 revision has remained AACR2. ACOC was firmly of the view that what would be unacceptable to the Australian library community would be a comprehensive revision of the rules—an AACR3. Not only would this not be acceptable, it was also considered to be not necessary. But a mechanism for maintenance is essential even if the amount of maintenance needed is minimal.

And in the same way that the JSC has proved to be an effective mechanism for achieving change, ACOC is considered to have proved to be an effective consultative mechanism for processing Australian input, and it would hope to be able to continue that role.

ACOC was moved to recommend that the revision process could be more structured and deliberate, although my experience suggests that it is principally up to JSC to develop a *modus operandi* that will best suit its changing corporate character.

For future JSC meetings ACOC does in fact have an unfinished agenda of rule revision proposals. They cover much the same scope of topics taken to the earlier JSC meetings inasmuch as they range from the provocative to the small, but nonetheless significant, improvements. ACOC proposes to continue to act as a filtering mechanism using its political nous and technical expertise to evaluate not only the practicality but also the acceptability of proposals as rule revisions.

Australian Representation

The constituency on which the Australian Committee on Cataloguing draws for input to the rule revision process is very much smaller than that on which the American and British representatives draw and somewhat smaller than that which the Canadian representative has behind him or her. The Australian constituency would also appear to be generally quite restrained, although not entirely devoid of the somewhat brash national character. The constituency does, however, recognize that we have made contact with the previously unknown, that our ideas are accepted as having merit and deserving of professional consideration, that there is a mechanism for effective input, that the opportunity is real and manageable.

To the representative on the JSC, the committee that is being represented becomes even more important than the broader constituency behind that. And the dynamics of the committees behind the representatives would appear to be quite strikingly different. I was always most fortunate to have a very understanding group that appreciated that, while trusting me to do my best to put across the ACOC position, at times I had to exercise my personal judgment in the JSC meetings. I felt—as the representative of the newcomer on the block at JSC meetings—that I was never entirely party to a number of the political strands that had their roots in days long passed. And, as a random observation, I think some aspects of the proceedings emphasized the fascinating often small, but nonetheless significant, national differences between people who speak (essentially) the same language.

The position of the Australian JSC representative is an elected one, for a three-year renewable term. Nominations are called for by the Australian Library and Information Association (formerly called the Library Association of Australia); ACOC considers and votes on the nominations, and their recommendation goes to the National Library of Australia and the Association for their ratification. I had the very real privilege of representing Australia on the JSC for six years, and I am particularly grateful to the State Library of New South Wales for underwriting my involvement. I recognize that it is perhaps unfortunate when committees have an almost complete change in membership at one time, although often strength comes from that as well. It was an opportune time for me to hand over the role of representing Australia, and I am delighted to have handed over to Diana Dack of the National Library of Australia, who I am confident will represent Australia very well as the JSC sets itself on a new path following the 1988 revision.

I imagine that the temptation has always been present for librarians, along with other professionals, to be sure that the environment that they are currently working in is more demanding, more complex, etc., than that experienced by previous generations. But it is most difficult to believe that this is not true for now. The pressures for accountability, the challenges of technological innovation, the attacks on funding for "public good" services, and the drive for quality customer service all impact on cataloging. There is a significant drive to see cataloging achieved as efficiently as possible, as a technical process with attention firmly focused on the access issues—the delivery side. And, meanwhile, the bibliographic databases built on these cataloging rules are becoming more central to the library's services, as more varied data and increasingly sophisticated functions are integrated into them. Those involved with rule revision need to remain cognizant of the environment in which catalogers are operating; but they are still primarily concerned with the standard, and the standard remains as necessary as ever. They are charged with honing the standard to enable librarians to take the rules on board and use them appropriately for their purpose—in line with their library's mission. Little credit will accrue to catalogers if, in approving revised standards, they are just seen as being efficient at moving around the deckchairs on the *Titanic*, and catalogers have to recognize the importance of retaining the respect of library management and of continuing to communicate with them—the discussion of cataloging confined to taking place just between catalogers circumscribes the definition of cataloging. My assessment is that Australia's involvement in the JSC has made a worthwhile contribution to Australia's having faced these challenges realistically and with confidence as part of the international community.

Notes

1. Alan Horton, "Cataloguing Is Too Important to Be Left to the Cataloguers," *Cataloguing Australia* 6, no. 3 (1980): 10–25.
2. Olivia Abbay, "Pseudonyms: Changing the Rules," *Cataloguing Australia* 13, no. 1 (1987): 17–22.

AACR2: Implementation and Interpretation of 1988 Revision

Ben R. Tucker

The reception of the 1978 publication we call AACR2 was largely un-favorable during the two years that passed before its adoption in January of 1981. These two years provided an opportunity for those who had just learned of the changes to make predictions that were engaged but not necessarily informed. For a while there were real difficulties in proceeding with plans for adoption, because directors of large research libraries were concerned, not only over the expense they foresaw in making any necessary changes, but also because their budgets were already showing signs of the shrinkage that became severe in the 1980s. The anxiety over "the strange new cataloging rules" was extreme in some cases, leading to predictions that the rules would wreck existing catalogs and thereby greatly interfere with existing ready access to huge library collections.

Although most of these dire predictions did not come true, nevertheless when the 1988 revision was being planned, a new wave of anxiety surfaced over "yet another new rule book." Happily, this most recent concern was less extreme than before and has been easily answered with hard facts. The chief fact to be noted is how little in the 1988 revision is "new." A close examination of the volume provides ready proof. For starters, there are the new options in the rules for bibliographic description, e.g., those for paral-lelisms. None of these options breaks new ground, and indeed we have found that despite heavy publicizing of all the new options (e.g., the tentative decisions published in *Cataloging Service Bulletin*), it has been virtually impossible to spark any interest in them. This response is in marked contrast with that directed at the options in the 1978 publication: the first round of meetings for implementation following publication was devoted to the options and alternative rules.

What is generally new is to find inside this "new" book all the rule revisions since 1981, together with some Library of Congress interpretations. It is to be hoped that this novelty will be seen as really beneficial and a cause for happiness rather than anxiety. Indeed, such changes as those for pseudonyms, British places, or serial titles are a cause for rejoicing. They are not new since they were publicized and adopted well before publication in the 1988 revision, after being almost universally supported at every step from proposal to final approval.

Together with a new volume made up primarily of "old" rules, an essential partner in good rule application is the cataloger. Much has been said recently about educating, recruiting, training, and, most of all, relying on the professional judgment of these workers. In an ideal world, the rule book and the cataloger would be sufficient, but in cataloging, life is neither ideal nor fair. Not every cataloger has been professionally trained; not all recruited catalogers receive equal or adequate on-the-job training, each library having its own practices to follow and preserve; the bibliographical world continues to evolve, requiring that new or changed phenomena be addressed, even though the rule book is supposedly "finished," at least for the moment. Another inescapable fact is that catalogers are increasingly either contributing to national databases or needing to be compatible with them, and they therefore need to know about interpretations and policies of application. There is inevitably a demonstrable need for more documentation on rule application, whatever the quality of either the rules or the catalogers.

Library of Congress Rule Interpretations is the specific ancillary documentation for AACR2 that is of the greatest concern to most United States catalogers. Interpretations are only a part of this series of documents, since it is also the medium for decisions about options, alternative rules, and various other rules that invite choices at the institutional rather than the cataloger level. Also included are interim rule revisions and some routines to be followed by Library of Congress catalogers when searching or in taking certain actions related to rule application at the Library. For the narrow category commonly referred to as interpretation, these documents are not produced routinely and do not represent a systematic treatment of the rules. When problems are addressed in a way that it is felt other catalogers would benefit, the solution is written up as an interpretation. A certain amount of discrimination is called for since catalogers are quite naturally full of questions; most of the answers are *ad hoc* and need not be preserved and shared with others. Despite shrinking budgets, the Library of Congress still has many, many catalogers and a wide cataloging program involving most of the materials covered by AACR2. This entails heavy use of the rules, and hence requires more interpretation than in any other library; certainly there is no national library that produces a similar number or range of bibliographic records, especially since almost all of them focus overwhelmingly on its own country's production.

Anyone can suggest a rule interpretation, whether that person is a Library of Congress staff member or not. Over the years they have been suggested by catalogers, administrators, reference librarians, and others. However, most are generated normally in the course of the cataloger's work, where the problem turns up. From time to time, the result is a formal interpretation. The Office for Descriptive Cataloging Policy drafts the document, which is then circulated to the affected units within the Library of Congress, to all Name Authority Cooperative Project (NACO) and National Coordinated Cataloging Program (NCCP) libraries, and also to OCLC Online Computer Library Center, Research Libraries Information Network (RLIN), and the Western (formerly Washington) Library Network (WLN). The final version evolves through a lengthy, democratic process of comments, further drafts, and consultations as necessary, with eventual publication in the series issued by the Cataloging Distribution Service.

Since the interpretations are finally published and distributed widely, they are adopted almost to the extent of the adoption of the rule book itself. Within the United States at least, there is generally as close an adherence to them as to the rules. They are nonetheless not "rules." As explained above, they are ancillary statements supplementing the rules, as they are used in one national library. In nature they are usually more specific than the rules, often approaching a cataloging manual. The rules themselves are a general code, agreed to by official representatives of the United States, Australia, the United Kingdom, and Canada.

One can ask: Is there life for AACR2 after interpretation and other actions by the Library of Congress? The answer is: Of course. Look at the history of rule revision, in which we are all involved, and how much it has depended on and profited from several years of deliberation with the Committee on Cataloging: Description and Access. What we have is a living code constantly in use, a code that is responsive to changing conditions and needs.

So what does the future hold? Let me hazard some guesses:

1. I foresee very few changes in the rules for form of heading. Neither you nor we can bear this type of revision, except in major cases of overwhelming need (and expense be damned!), such as pseudonyms and British place names;
2. There will be some fine-tuning of rules for choice of main entry heading;
3. There will be *a lot* of fine-tuning of the rules for bibliographic description.

It all should sound harmless, but it is sure to cause alarm in some quarters. Such a thought leads me to my conclusion, which is that the history of our rule book will continue to be an always interesting dialectic contest between lively innovation and tenacious conservatism.

Bibliographic Description and Changes in Chapters 1, 2, 4, and 12

Olivia M. A. Madison

The majority of all materials cataloged according to the *Anglo-American Cataloguing Rules,* second edition, 1988 revision (AACR2R) are described according to rules contained in chapters 1, 2, and 12. Chapter 1 is the general chapter that provides the umbrella of rules for all materials. Chapters 2 and 12 are the specific chapters for books and serials. Because of the heavy use of these chapters by the cataloging community, the revisions contained in them were of intense interest to that community. What effect would the changes found in these chapters coupled with those changes in AACR2R's access-related chapters have on cataloging? Of particular concern were the future costs associated with time and effort required for cataloging, along with the maintenance of local catalogs, shared catalogs, and the databases of the bibliographic utilities. Because many of the revisions had been issued over time, it was clear to catalogers aware of those changes that the revisions were minor in nature.

Below, the major revisions contained in these three chapters are described, along with those in chapter 4 (manuscripts and manuscript collections). Most of these revisions are simplifications or editorial corrections of existing rules, such as simplification of playing time, or revision to the serial frequency note. Some few constitute expansions of existing provisions, such as the expansion of the list of general material designations (GMDs) and more detailed provisions for multiple publishers, distributors, etc.

The discussion that follows is in four segments, for chapters 1, 2, 4, and 12 of AACR2R, respectively. For revisions to chapter 1 that involve other chapters, the details of those changes are described in the workshop-based chapters dealing with the other descriptive chapters.

Chapter 1. General Comments

Chapter 1 provides the general framework for the bibliographic description of all materials, while the individual descriptive chapters contain the specific rules necessary to describe successfully specific types of materials. The major revisions in chapter 1 primarily deal with provisions for the optional transcription of parallel data, the addition of several new general material designations and qualifying terms, expanded description for braille and other raised types, and simplification of playing times.

1.1B10. Collective Title and the Titles of Individual Works

While the directive in rule 1.1B10 regarding what to do when the chief source of information bears both a collective title and the titles of individual works is not new to AACR2R, it is new to chapter 1. Previously the rule was located in chapter 2 as rule 2.1B2. Because materials other than books, pamphlets, and printed sheets may contain a collective title coupled with titles of individual works, the Joint Steering Committee for Revision of AACR (JSC) moved the rule to chapter 1 (*see* figures 1 and 2).

1.1C1. Optional Addition. General Material Designation

The general material designation (GMD) is a term used to describe a broad type of material to which specific types of items might belong. For example, the GMD that a cataloger would use for either an item that is a reel of microfilm or an item that is a microfiche would be the more general term "microform." When used, the GMD follows the title proper. While the GMD is an optional provision, it is a useful descriptive mechanism to notify the user of the general format of the item.

AACR2R provides two lists for the selection of an appropriate GMD. List 1 is used by cataloging agencies in the United Kingdom. In list 1 the GMD "braille" was added, and "machine-readable data file" was replaced by the GMD "computer file." List 2, a more extensive list, is used by cataloging agencies in Australia, Canada, and the United States. In list 2 the GMDs "art reproduction," "toy," and "braille" were added and "machine-readable data file" also was replaced by the GMD "computer file." In addition, the qualifying terms "(large print)," "(tactile)," and "(braille)"

Monograph title page:

THREE PIONEERING EGYPTIAN NOVELS
The Maiden of Dinshway (1906), Eve without Adam (1934),
and Ulysses's Hallucinations or the Like (1985)

Translated with a Critical Introduction
by SAAD EL-GABALAWY

Title and statement of responsibility:

> Three pioneering Egyptian novels /
> translated with a critical introduction by
> Saad El-Gabalawy.

Contents note:

> Contents: The maiden of Dinshway (1906)
> -- Eve without Adam (1934) -- Ulysses's
> hallucinations or the like (1985)

Figure 1.   Collective Title and Titles of Individual Works

Compact disc (partial data from disc):

David Sanborn

Hideaway

1. Hideaway
2. Carly's Song
3. Anything You Want
4. The Seduction (Love Theme)
5. Lisa
6. IF YOU WOULD BE MINE
7. Creeper
8. Again An' Again

Title and statement of responsibility:

> Hideaway [sound recording] / David Sanborn.

Contents note:

> Contents: Hideaway -- Carly's song --
> Anything you want -- The seduction (love
> theme) -- Lisa -- If you would be mine --
> Creeper -- Again an' again.

Figure 2.   Collective Title and Individual Works

were added for qualifying any term in list 2, with the exception of the GMDs "braille" or "text."

Most of the GMD revisions were part of an entire set of revisions found throughout Part I that deal with more precise revisions associated with material for the visually impaired. These revisions were initiated by the Canadian Committee on Cataloguing in response to the need for a more detailed level of bibliographic description for material intended for the visually impaired.

1.3. Material (or Type of Publication) Specific Details Area

Rule 1.3 provides a reference to those Part I chapters that provide for the use of a material-specific detail area. The use of this area was expanded in AACR2R. Three references were added for the following types of materials: music (chapter 5), computer files (chapter 9), and, in some cases, microforms (chapter 11). Previously AACR2 used this area only for cartographic materials and serial publications. Specific examples of the expanded use of this area are found in the workshop chapters for computer files, music, and microforms.

1.4C5. Two or More Places of Publication, Distribution, Etc.

The revision found in rule 1.4C5 is an excellent example of how the rule revision process is truly part of the cataloging community family. As way of background, the revision process for rule 1.4C5 began in a cataloging class taught by Arlene Taylor. It was continued by Arlene Taylor and Richard Smiraglia through ALA's Committee on Cataloging: Description and Access (CC:DA), and ended with the JSC revising the rule. Quite simply, it took a cataloging student to discover that a rule was not what the cataloging community thought it was. Specifically, AACR2 rule 1.4C5 stated "If a publisher, distributor, etc., has offices in more than one place and these are named in the item, give the first named place, and any subsequently named place that is in the home country of the cataloguing agency or is given prominence by the layout of the source of information. Omit all other places."[1]

Therefore, if the following information concerning the place of publication was given in the chief source of information:

```
Chicago   New York   London
```

AACR2 instructed a cataloger in the United States to give the place of publication as:

```
Chicago ; New York
```

AACR2R now states "If two or more places in which a publisher, distributor, etc., has offices are named in the item, give the first named place. Give any subsequently named place that is given prominence . . . ."[2] Therefore, for a cataloging agency in the United States, the above example would read:

```
Chicago
```

1.4D5. Two or More Publishers, Distributors, Etc.

Rule 1.4D5 was greatly expanded in order to specify the cases in which more than one publisher, distributor, etc., is named in a bibliographic description. While AACR2 stated that a subsequently named body should be named only if it was given prominence by typography, AACR2R now gives four cases when it would be appropriate to add an additional publisher, distributor, etc. Those four cases are as follows:

1. "when the first and subsequently named entities are linked in a single statement"[3]

Example:

```
[London] : Longman with the Local
    Government Training Board
```

2. "when the first named entity is a distributor, releasing agency, etc., and a publisher is named subsequently"[4]

Example:

```
London ; New York : Royal Institute of
    International Affairs : Routledge & Kegan
    Paul
```

3. "when a subsequently named entity is clearly distinguished as the principal publisher, distributor, etc., by layout or typography"[5]

This provision is essentially the content of the former rule contained in AACR2.

4. "when the subsequently named publisher, distributor, etc., is in the home country of the cataloguing agency and the first named publisher, distributor, etc., is not."[6]

This specific provision is parallel in intent to the aforementioned revised Rule 1.4D5.

Example for a cataloging agency in the United States:

```
Glasgow : Blackier ; New York : Chapman and
    Hall
```

1.5B4. Playing Time

The rules for recording playing time now no longer expect the cataloger to time the playing time of a motion picture, sound recording, etc. Instead, preference is given to what the item states is the playing time, and the time given in the description should be what is stated on the item. If the item does not give a stated playing time, the rules suggest recording an approximate time.

In addition, rule 1.5B4 contains an optional rule for parts of a multi-part item when those parts are given a stated or approximate uniform playing time. In these cases, one may record the playing time in one of the two ways:

```
8 film reels (40 min. each)
```

or

```
8 film reels (320 min.)
```

1.5D2. Container Dimensions

AACR2R now provides an option in rule 1.5D2 that permits recording the dimensions of the container, whether alone or in conjunction with the dimensions of the items it contains.

1.7A4 and 1.7B22. Notes for Reproductions and Original

Rule 1.7A4 was expanded to provide directions on how to give notes for reproductions. It now states that notes regarding the reproduction are given first, and the notes relating to the original are combined into one note with the details given "in the order of the areas to which they relate."[7] The specifics of how the note regarding the original would appear is given in rule 1.7B22.

1.7B. Order of Notes

AACR2 stated that notes should be given in the order they are listed in the rules. However, AACR2R states that while notes should be given in the order in which they are listed, a particular note may be given first if it has been decided that it is of primary importance. CC:DA began discussing the order of notes in response to a memorandum from Ben Tucker of the Library of Congress to CC:DA. The memorandum stated that the Canadian Committee on Cataloguing had taken the Library of Congress "to task for recording the publisher's numbers found on sound recordings as the first note rather than the last."[8] He further noted that LC merely was following the express wish of sound recording librarians and asked that the appropriate CC:DA liaisons restate the arguments in light of their experience with the AACR2. Following that discussion, he suggested that CC:DA consider whether or not rule revision for sound recordings was necessary. Instead of a specific rule revision for rule 6.5B2, CC:DA recommended to JSC that it generalize the question to whenever circumstances warrant a change in the order of notes for any type of material that it should be allowed. JSC concurred with the CC:DA's recommendation and revised rule 1.7B to allow a different order of notes. In terms of the rule's application, there was general consensus within the previous CC:DA discussion that, because of the enormous use of shared cataloging through the bibliographic utilities, any change in the order of notes contained in shared records should be in accordance with general agreement within the national cataloging community. As a result of this revision, the sound recording publisher's number continues to be given as the first note.

Chapter 2. Books, Pamphlets, and Printed Sheets

AACR2R chapter 2 contains the rules for the bibliographic description of printed monographs, referred to as books, pamphlets, and printed sheets. This chapter does not contain many revisions, and this section will review only one revision. However, of note is that the rules now provide provisions to add more detailed physical characteristics for braille, other raised type, and large print intended for the visually impaired (rules 2.5B23 and 2.5B24).

2.0B2. Prescribed Sources of Information

AACR2R contains one change for determining which data are used as the prescribed source of information for series information. Previously the rules stated that the source was the whole publication. This rather open-ended information source led to differences in choice of what could be used as the series statement. In need of a standard for the selection of series statements in the United States, the Library of Congress issued a rule interpretation that stated that the order of preference should be: the series title page, the monograph title page, or other integral sources. Rule 2.0B2, which covers the order of preference, provides more guidance as it calls for the series title page first, and then the monograph title page, the cover, and the rest of the publication (*see* figures 3 and 4).

Later on, it will be seen that this revision parallels the instructions for the use of title page substitutes for serials.

Chapter 4. Manuscripts
(including Manuscript Collections)

Because a variety of different formats may have material designated as manuscripts, chapter 4 is used in conjunction with the provisions found in other chapters used to describe unpublished items. The two revisions that

---

Cover:

> JPS GEMS OF AMERICAN JEWISH LITERATURE
> WASTELAND
> JO SINCLAIR
> INTRODUCTION BY VIVIAN GORNICK
> THE JEWISH PUBLICATION SOCIETY
> PHILADELPHIA NEW YORK JERUSALEM
> 1987

Monograph title page:

> GEMS OF AMERICAN JEWISH LITERATURE
> WASTELAND
> JO SINCLAIR
> INTRODUCTION BY VIVIAN GORNICK

Cataloging record (abbreviated):

```
Wasteland / Jo Sinclair ; introduction by
Vivian Gornick. -- Philadelphia : Jewish
Publication Society, 1987.

395 p. ; 35 cm. -- (Gems of American
Jewish literature)
```

Figure 3.   Choice of Series Title

Cover:

> PACIFIC AND WORLD STUDIES, NO. 1

Monograph title page:

> PACIFIC AND WORLD STUDIES, NO. 1

Series title page:

> PACIFIC AND WORLD STUDIES SERIES

Series statement:

> (Pacific and world studies series ; no. 1)

Figure 4.   Prescribed Sources of Information—Series

are discussed deal with the recognition by JSC that manuscripts may have edition statements.

4.0B2. Prescribed Sources of Information

Under AACR2R rule 4.0B2 (the designated sources of information), the edition area now is listed, with its prescribed source of information being the chief source of information. The chief source is the manuscript itself, and within a manuscript, the order of preference is the title page, the colophon, the caption, heading, etc., or the content of the manuscript. If sources within the original manuscript are not available, the rules provide further sources. Finally, for a collection of manuscripts, the whole collection is the chief source of information.

Rule 4.0B2 of AACR2R states that if the chief source of information is not used for the transcription of the edition area, then the cataloger should use published copies of the manuscript.

4.2B. Edition Statement
4.2C. Statements of Responsibility Relating to the Edition

The edition area contains specific instructions for the transcription of the actual edition statement (*see* figure 5), which includes the possibility of a statement of responsibility associated with a given edition statement. The rule further states that if the cataloger is not certain whether or not a statement is an actual edition statement, the statement should not be included in this area. Furthermore, if an item does not include an edition statement, but the cataloger is certain that the item contains significant changes from

Manuscript title page:

DRAFT 2
Faculty Council History Committee
IOWA STATE UNIVERSITY FACULTY COUNCIL, 1954–1988
A History
By
Olivia M. A. Madison
Wayne S. Osborn
Rae Haws
Edited by Carol S. David
1988 April

Cataloging record:

```
Madison, Olivia M. A.
  Iowa State University Faculty Council,
1954-1988 : a history / by Olivia M. A. Madi-
son, Wayne S. Osborn, Rae Haws ; edited by
Carol S. David. -- Draft 2. -- 1988 Apr.

  At head of title:  Faculty Council History
Committee.
```

Figure 5.   Manuscript Edition Statement

other "editions," then an appropriate statement may be supplied in square brackets.

Chapter 12. Serials

Chapter 12 for serials provides the descriptive rules for serial publications of all formats. The chapter is intended to be used in conjunction with the other Part I chapters that deal with the corresponding physical formats possible for serials. As indicated earlier for monographs and manuscripts, the descriptive rules for serials were not changed substantially in AACR2R. Perhaps the most important revision was the changes found in the rules for the sources of information. These rules were modified and made parallel with the corresponding rules in chapter 2. In addition, there was an important clarification made in the rules regarding the transcription of initialisms and acronyms. There also were minor revisions associated with the specific material designation for printed serials and the example used for the frequency note.

12.0B1. Sources of Information for Printed Serials

AACR2R calls for a different order for selecting the title page substitute than was found in AACR2. If the serial being cataloged does not contain a title page for the first issue of the serial or a title page for the first available issue, the cataloger is to turn to the title page substitute. Now the first choice is the analytical title page. The prescribing of the analytical title page as the first title page substitute makes this rule parallel to rule 2.0B2, which was described earlier (*see* figure 6). Even with this revision there is still controversy within the serials cataloging community over what should be given preference as a title page substitute. Of particular concern is the preference for the cover, which some serial catalogers believe is very "unstable" in continuity, and they believe the contents page would be more reliable in format and "stability" (*see* figure 7).

The following is the list of the title page substitutes for both sets of rules:

AACR2	**AACR2R**
Cover	Analytical title page
Caption	Cover
Masthead	Caption
Editorial pages	Masthead
Colophon	Editorial pages
Other pages	Colophon
	Other pages

Cover:

JAAR Thematic Studies 48/3 & 4
Charisma and Sacred Biography
Edited by Michael A. Williams
A Thematic Series of the Journal of the
American Academy of Religion Studies

Analytical title page:

Charisma and Sacred Biography
Edited by Michael A. Williams
Journal of the American Academy of Religion Studies
Volume XLVIII, Numbers 3 and 4

Choice of serial title:

```
Journal of the American Academy of Religion
Studies
```

Figure 6.   Chief Source of Information for Printed Serials

Cover:

> Criminology & Penology Abstracts

Serial contents page:

> Criminology and Penology Abstracts

Choice of serial title proper:

```
Criminology & penology abstracts
```

Figure 7.   Chief Source of Information for Printed Serials

12.1B2. Full Form/Acronym or Initialism
12.1E1. Note on Full Form/Acronym or Initialism

Chapter 12 contains revisions pertaining to the choice of title and the types of notes that should be expected in cases when a serial publication contains both a full form of a title as well as an acronym or initialism of that title. These particular revisions arose out of a rule revision proposed to CC:DA by the Committee to Study Serials Cataloging of the ALA Serials Section. The purpose of the proposed revision was to "legalize" an existing Library of Congress rule interpretation. CC:DA supported the proposal and submitted it to the JSC, which concurred with the need to clarify the rules regarding this often confusing bibliographic situation.

Rule 12.1B2 now states that when a title "appears in full and in the form of an acronym or initialism in the chief source of information, choose the full form as the title proper unless the acronym or initialism is the only form of title presented in other locations in the serial" [9] (*see* figure 8). Correspondingly, rule 12.1E1 instructs that when an acronym or initialism and its full

Cover:

> MCSS
> MATHEMATICS OF CONTROL, SIGNALS, AND SYSTEMS

Spine title:

> MATHEMATICS OF CONTROL, SIGNALS, AND SYSTEMS

Choice of serial title proper and other title information:

```
Mathematics of control, signals, and sys-
tems : MCSS
```

Figure 8.   Initialism/Acronym or Full Form of Title

form appear in the chief source of information, the cataloger should transcribe as other title information the form not selected as the title proper.

12.1B7. Title Proper Changes

Chapter 12 now contains linkage to chapter 21 in that rule 12.1B8 states that a cataloger should make a new description when a title proper changes, and refers the cataloger to rule 21.2C. While this directive was generally understood by serials catalogers, the reference provides a useful reminder.

12.5B1. Extent of Item (Including Specific Material Designation)

The specific material designations given in rule 12.5B1 were expanded for serials. Now "no." and "pt." may be used in addition to "v."

12.7B1. Frequency Notes

While there was no rule revision associated with rule 12.7B1, the "nonprescriptive" example for a changed frequency statement was revised. The following two examples demonstrate the revised nonprescriptive note.
AACR2

```
Six issues yearly (1950-1961), monthly
   (1962- )10
```

AACR2R

```
Six issues yearly, 1950-1961; monthly,
   1962- 11
```

Conclusion

The revisions contained in chapters 1, 2, 4, and 12 were primarily editorial or expansionary in nature. Many of the revisions regularize the choices used for recording bibliographic data. The revisions contained in the rules for the prescribed sources of information were made primarily to standardize where catalogers should obtain bibliographic data. Other revisions, such as those regarding place and publisher transcriptions, standardize what transcribed data are found in the publication, distribution, etc., areas. One important revision, that regarding the recording of playing time, was based on the guiding principle of AACR2—cataloging should be based on the item in hand.

While the revisions were not major revolutionary changes, they were meant to standardize and simplify descriptive cataloging based on AACR2R. In this they have succeeded.

Notes

1. *Anglo-American Cataloguing Rules,* 2d ed. (Chicago: American Library Association, 1978), 32 (hereafter cited as *AACR2*).
2. *Anglo-American Cataloguing Rules,* 2d ed., 1988 revision (Chicago: American Library Association, 1988), 35–36 (hereafter cited as *AACR2R*).
3. *AACR2R,* 38.
4. *AACR2R,* 38.
5. *AACR2R,* 38.
6. *AACR2R,* 38.
7. *AACR2R,* 50.
8. Ben R. Tucker, Memorandum to Olivia Madison, Chairman, CC:DA, on sound recording publishers' numbers as first note, April 5, 1985.
9. *AACR2R,* 278.
10. *AACR2,* 262.
11. *AACR2R,* 291.

Changes to
Chapters 3, 5, 6, 7, 8, 10, and 11

Ben R. Tucker and Edward Swanson

This chapter covers the changes made to those chapters in AACR2 that deal with nonprint materials other than manuscripts and computer files, namely cartographic materials, music, sound recordings, motion pictures and video-recordings, graphic materials, three-dimensional artefacts and realia, and microforms.

Chapter 3. Cartographic Materials

The first major change made to chapter 3 relates to the scope of the chapter itself. While cartographic materials are found in collections that tradition-ally treat them as cartographic materials, they also are found in other collections such as media centers, learning centers, and school libraries where the emphasis is placed on using the items as aids to teaching rather than primarily as maps.

These items might be in the form of traditional maps, but equally they might be in the form of posters, flash cards, filmstrips, etc., and the institution cataloging them is treating them not as cartographic materials *per se* but as teaching tools. In the review that led to the publication of the 1988 revision it was found that the "map" librarian has good reason for wanting to treat such items as cartographic materials, while the "audiovisual" librar-ian has equally good reasons for treating them as audiovisual items.

A new sentence was added at the end of rule 3.0A1 to deal with items that present cartographic information but that are in a physical form that falls within the scope of another chapter. The cataloger is instructed to consult the rules in chapter 3 in conjunction with the rules in the chapter appropriate to the form of the material. It also is understood that the same item can be cataloged equally as a cartographic item (using a specific material designation in area 5 such as "1 map") or as an exemplar of its physical format, using a specific material designation for that format in area 5 (e.g., "1 jigsaw puzzle").

Although no change was made to rule 3.1C relating to the general material designation used for cartographic materials, it should be pointed out that rule 0.25, which in the 1978 edition allowed for repeating area 3 for serial cartographic materials, has been generalized to apply to other types of materials as well (e.g., serial computer files).

One of the early changes made to area 3 in chapter 3 was the revision of rule 3.3D2, which greatly expanded the rules for stating the coordinates of celestial charts. The rule in the 1978 edition lacked the detail now provided; in addition it contained some inaccuracies. This change was made shortly after the adoption of AACR2 in 1981, and it was published in the 1983 packet of rule revisions.

Probably the most extensively revised section of chapter 3 is the sequence of rules for the physical description area. In the 1978 edition, rule 3.5B1 provided twenty-six separate specific material designations for describing the extent of a cartographic item. The fine distinctions necessary with such a multiplicity of terms proved impractical for most catalogers. When the Anglo-American cartographic cataloging manual, *Cartographic Materials,* was published in 1982, the list was reduced to nine terms; this list was carried over into the 1988 revision.

The term "section" was and still is part of the name of one of the specific material designations, "map section." In the 1978 edition, "section" also was used in the statement of extent in area 5 to indicate that a map appeared in multiple pieces or parts. There was considerable confusion over using the same term both for a particular type of map and for a map appearing in multiple parts.

In the 1988 revision it was decided to confine the use of "section" to its cartographic sense in "map section." This is defined in the glossary as

> A scale representation of a vertical surface (commonly a plane) displaying both the profile where it intersects the surface of the ground, or some conceptual model, and the underlying structures along the plane of intersection (e.g., a geological section).[1]

When the intent is to express the fact that the map appears in pieces, the 1988 revision instructs in rule 3.5B2 that the term "segment" is to be used (*see* figure 1, example A). Thus the two concepts are expressed in different terms.

There are two examples in the 1988 revision that did not get corrected in the process of changing the existing examples to match the new use of "section" and "segment." The first is the third example under the second paragraph of rule 3.5B4. This example also includes another error, namely the omission of the preposition "in" or "on" that must begin each specific material designation formulated under the second paragraph of rule 3.5B2. The example probably best is corrected by restating it as "on 2 segments of 2 maps in 6 segments" (cf. the example as it appeared in the 1978 text, "in 2 sections of 2 maps in sections").

The second erroneous example is the third example under the first paragraph in rule 3.5B5, the correction of which is obvious, "1 map in 4

At top: **CHILE**
At bottom:

Lambert Conformal Projection
Standard parallels 24°00′ and 49°00′
Scale 1:10,500,000; inset 1:30,000,000
Boundary representation is
not necessarily authoritative

[The map itself comprises an inset plus the northern half of Chile and the southern half of Chile]

                                    EXAMPLE A

```
    Chile [map]. -- Scale 1:10,500,000. --
[United States? : s.n., 198-?].
    1 map in 2 segments : col. ; 55 x 30 cm.

    Includes inset showing complete country of
Chile.  Scale: 1:30,000,000.
```

                                    EXAMPLE B

```
    Chile [map]. -- Scale 1:10,500,000. --
[United States? : s.n., 198-?].
    1 map : col. ; 55 x 30 cm.

    Map in 2 segments.
    Includes inset showing complete country of
Chile.  Scale: 1:30,000,000.
```

Figure 1.   Map in Segments

segments (print, braille and tactile)" (according to the *Chicago Manual of Style,* there should also be a comma following "braille").

As mentioned above, rule 3.5B2 provides that "in" and "on" phrases be added to the specific material designation when multiple maps are on a single sheet or when a single map is in more than one piece. The 1988 revision retains the stipulation for these additions, but an option for dropping them and giving that information in a note instead has been added (*see* figure 1, example B).

The final major change made to chapter 3 was the inclusion in rule 3.5B5 of the terms used for braille or other tactile systems used by the blind and visually impaired. These terms are given as parenthetical qualifiers of the specific material designation. The inclusion of these terms follows on the addition of rule 2.5B23, since the physical production of maps largely follows the same processes that are applied to printed texts.

Chapter 5. Music

Probably the most significant of the changes to chapter 5 was the rewriting of rule 5.1B1 to incorporate the information from rule 5.1B2 in the 1978 version. The result is that the cataloger now has a single rule to refer to when dealing with an extremely common phenomenon in cataloging music materials, namely deciding whether the beginning of a musical title can stand alone as the title proper, or whether it must be supported by the additional wording that ordinarily is considered to be other title information (*see* figures 2–4). According to all reports, the result of this rewriting is much clearer than previously.

There are two other major changes made to chapter 5. The first is the addition of area 3 to chapter 5 to provide for recording information about the "musical presentation" of the item. The "musical presentation statement" is defined as

> A term or phrase found in the chief source of information of a publication of printed music or a music manuscript that indicates the physical presentation of the music (e.g., score, miniature score, score and parts). This type of statement should be distinguished from one that indicates an arrangement or edition of a musical work (e.g., vocal score, 2-piano edition, version with orchestra accompaniment, chorus score).[2]

Title page:

MOZART

SYMPHONY NO. 40
G MINOR (K 550)

M. BARON, INC. NEW YORK

At bottom of each page of music: MB 17

```
Symphony no. 40, G minor, K 550 [music]
/ Mozart. -- New York : M. Baron, [19- ].
51 p. ; 21 cm.

Pl. no.: MB 17.
```

Figure 2.   Title Proper for Music

Title page:

EDITION PETERS
No. 3777

TSCHAIKOWSKY
TRIO
Klavier, Violine und Violoncello

Opus 50

At foot of each page of music: 10317

```
Trio, Klavier, Violine, und Violoncello,
opus 50 [music] / Tschaikowsky. —
[Leipzig] : Edition Peters, [1928].

Publisher's no.: Edition Peters no.
3777.  Pl. no.: 10317.
```

Figure 3.   Publisher's and Plate Numbers

In figure 4, the word "Partitur" indicates that the music has the physical format of a score. Likewise, in figure 5, "Piano et chant" indicates the musical presentation of that item.

Both the revision to rule 5.1B1 and the addition of area 3 were made early in the course of rule revision, being published in the 1982 and 1983 revision packets respectively, so their provisions were already being applied by the time the 1988 revision was published.

The other major change made to chapter 5 was the revision of rule 5.7B19. In the 1978 edition, the cataloger was instructed to record the plate

Title page:

Boris Blacher

Op. 38

Divertimento
für vier Holzbläser
Flöte, Oboe, Klarinette, Fagott

Partitur

[Publisher's emblem]
Gegründet 1838

Ed. Bote & G. Bock, Berlin-Wiesbaden
For U.S.A., Canada & Mexico: Assoc. Music Publishers, Inc., New
York

At foot of first page of music:

Copyright 1951 by Ed. Bote & G. Bock, Berlin
assigned to Association Music Publishers, Inc., New York
B. & B.
30960

```
     Divertimento für vier Holzbläser, Flöte,
Oboe, Klarinette, Fagott, op. 38 [music]
/ Boris Blacher. -- Partitur. -- Berlin : Ed.
Bode & G. Bock ; New York : Assoc. Music
Publishers, c1951.

     1 miniature score (24 p.) ; 22 cm.

     Duration: ca. 10:00.
     Publisher's no.: B. & B. 30960.
```

Figure 4.   Musical Presentation

number found on the item. If no plate number was given, then the cataloger
was to record the publisher's number.

In the 1988 revision, the cataloger now is instructed to record both the
plate number and the publisher's number if both appear on the item. Figures
2 and 5 illustrate recording of a plate number; figure 4 illustrates recording
a publisher's number; figure 3 illustrates recording both the plate number
and the publisher's number.

Unfortunately, there was one additional major change made to the rules
in chapter 5, albeit inadvertently during the course of handling the proofs
for printing. In rule 5.0B2, "first page of music" was omitted from the
prescribed sources of information for the publication, distribution, etc., area.

Title page:

ERIK SATIE
CHEZ LE DOCTEUR
PIANO et CHANT

EDITIONS SALABERT
22, rue Chauchat - PARIS
575 Madison Avenue and 57th Street - NEW YORK

In caption: Paroles de Vincent Hyspa

At foot of page 1:

© 1976 by Editions Salabert - Paris
E.A.S. 17209

International Copyright secured all rights reserved

EDITIONS SALABERT S.A. 22 rue Chauchat - PARIS

```
Chez le docteur [music] / Erik Satie ;
[paroles de Vincent Hyspa]. -- Piano et
chant. -- Paris ; New York : Editions
Salabert, 1976.
   3 p. ; 32 cm.

   Pl. no.: E.A.S. 17209.
```

Figure 5.   Musical Presentation

The result is that copyright dates almost always would be bracketed since they regularly appear at the bottom of the first page of music. The major cataloging agencies (e.g., the Library of Congress in the United States) have issued instructions to the effect that "first page of music" should continue to be considered as a prescribed source for this area, and the Joint Steering Committee for Revision of AACR is considering restoring this source.

Chapter 6. Sound Recordings

AACR2 broke with previous cataloging practice in a significant way. Under earlier cataloging rules, the sound recording label name and number had been given as the final element of the body of the description, rather than the place, publisher, and date as in records for other types of materials.

AACR2 provided for chapter 6 to conform to the International Standard for Bibliographic Description (ISBD) pattern for area 4, so that for the first time in the cataloging of sound recordings the regular information about publication began to appear in bibliographical records. This modification has held up remarkably well, and only two significant points specific to sound recordings came to the attention of the revisers of the rules since the adoption of AACR2 in 1981.

The first major change came about because of technological developments, namely the advent of the compact disc. The rules and examples in areas 5 and 7 of chapter 6 were modified to include provisions for cataloging CDs. In rule 6.5C2, a new rule was added instructing the cataloger to give the "type of recording (i.e., the way in which the sound is encoded on the item)"[3] (*see* figure 6). A new instruction was added to rule 6.5C3 for recording the speed of a digital disc in metres per second, together with an instruction for omitting this information if it is standard for the item (1.4 metres per second is standard for digital compact discs).

The inclusion of the instructions for these digital discs also entailed the correction of terms in the rules and examples to designate all cases dealing with non-digital sound recordings. For example, rule 6.5C2 now provides for designating a non-digital recording by the term "analog" (*see* figure 7).

The second major change relates to the gradual evolution of the importance of the phonogram date for sound recordings. In the 1978 edition, the regular copyright symbol, "c," had been used both for the regular copyright of art work, text, etc., on the container and for the special copyright that applies to the actual sound in the sound recording. The 1988 revision now allows for the use of the appropriate "p" symbol to represent the special copyright.

Three other significant changes were made in chapter 6 due to the revision of rules in other other chapters of Part I of AACR2. First, the provisions for recording playing time in rule 6.5B2 were removed and replaced with a reference to the instructions in rule 1.5B4. There had been a widely expressed need for an improvement in the rule for playing time, no matter whether films or sound recordings are involved, so rule 1.5B4 was added. The result is basically that the cataloger copies statements of duration from the item being cataloged.

Following up on the improvement made in rule 5.1B1 for determining the title proper of a music item, a reference to the rules in 5.1B was added to rule 6.1B1 for music sound recordings.

Old rule 6.11, which dealt with nonprocessed sound recordings (i.e., noncommercial instantaneous recordings that generally exist in unique copies), was deleted. General rules had been added to chapter 1 dealing with area 4 for nonpublished materials, and references were added to the rules in

On disc:

STAY
AWAKE
Various Interpretations of Music
from Vintage Disney Films

A&M   Produced by Hal Willner
RECORDS   for Deep Creek Productions, Ltd.
                                                  Executive Producers:
COMPACT   STEVE RALBOVSKY and
disc   HAL WILLNER
                                                        digital audio
                                            ℗ & © 1988 A&M Records, Inc.
aad   All rights reserved
                                                  A&M Records, Inc.
                                                      P.O. Box 118
                                                Hollywood, CA 90078
CD 3918   Made in U.S.A.
DIDX 003844
                          [Listing of contents]

On container:

ISBN 0-945338-21-X
[Bar code]: 0 7502-13918-2 6

Stay awake [sound recording] : various
interpretations of music from vintage
Disney films. -- Hollywood, CA : A&M
Records, p1988.

1 sound disc (66 min.) : digital ; 4
3/4 in.

A&M Records: CD 3918.
Performed by various artists.
Compact disc.
Contents: Opening medley : I'm
getting wet and I don't care at all
(9:02) -- Baby mine (3:14) -- Heigh-ho :
the Dwarfs' marching song (3:35) --
Medley two : The darkness sheds its veil
(7:47) -- Medley three : Three inches is
such a wretched height (5:57) -- Mickey
Mouse march (2:14) -- Medley four : All
innocent children had better beware
(15:15) -- Someday my prince will come
(1:08) -- Second star to the right
(4:01) -- Pinocchio medley (5:46).
ISBN 0-945338-21-X.

Figure 6.   Compact Disc

On container:

> In the Flesh: A Situation for Feminist Inquiry
> Hortense Spillers
> ICC Auditorium, June 20, 1986

```
    In the flesh [sound recording] : a
situation for feminist inquiry /
Hortense Spillers. -- 1986 June 20.
1 sound cassette : analog, mono.

Title from container.
Recorded June 20, 1986, in the ICC
Auditorium at Georgetown University.
```

Figure 7.   Unpublished Sound Recording

6.4 to cover nonpublished sound recordings. Basically, the rules in 1.4 instruct the cataloger to record only the date in area 4 for unpublished items (*see* figure 7).

Chapter 7. Motion Pictures and Videorecordings

Only one significant change was made to chapter 7, the move of technical information about a videorecording format (e.g., Beta, VHS) from a parenthetical qualifier of the specific material designation in area 5 to a note (rule 7.7B10) (*see* figure 8). The change resulted from the rewriting of chapter 9 and the placement, in that chapter, of technical specifications for software in the notes area. This probably has proved to be the one change in the 1988 revision that has caused the most unhappiness among users. Already considerable interest has been expressed in moving the information back to area 5. Until that is accomplished, however, it should be pointed out that some relief might be offered by the fact that the rules for notes in each of the chapters were changed to allow giving a particular note as the first note for a particular type of material when warranted.

As was true in chapter 6, references were added to the rules in 7.4 leading the cataloger back to the general rules in 1.4 for the treatment of area 4 for nonpublished motion pictures and videorecordings (*see* figure 8).

On label:

EastEnders—2/10/89-2/27/89

```
EastEnders [videorecording]. -- 1989
Feb. 10-1989 Feb. 27.
    1 videocassette (ca. 360 min.) ; sd.,
col. ; 1/2 in.

    Recording of broadcasts on KTCA-TV.
VHS format.
```

Figure 8.   Unpublished Videorecording

Chapter 8. Graphic Materials

In chapter 8, as in chapter 7, technical specifications were moved from area 5 to the notes area. Fortunately this change has not engendered the same storm of protest for the sake of materials covered by chapter 8. The only other change of any consequence was the consolidation of sixteen rules for recording other physical details, which are so different from medium to medium, into a single rule (8.5C2), and a rule for recording color characteristics was added.

Chapter 10. Three-dimensional Artefacts and Realia

Provisions were added to chapter 10 for dealing with braille and other tactile materials for the blind and visually impaired on the same basis as they were added to other chapters in Part I. In addition, the specific material designations "art original," "braille cassette," and "toy" were added.

Chapter 11. Microforms

The only major change made to chapter 11 came early in the rule revision process. In cases where the title is given in an abbreviated or shortened form on the header of a microfiche or a microopaque, and it appears in a fuller form on accompanying eye-readable material or the container, the eye-readable material or the container is to be treated as the chief source of information.

All other changes made to chapters 3, 5, 6, 7, 8, 10, and 11 were either editorial in nature or for clarification and are of minor significance.

Notes

1. *Anglo-American Cataloguing Rules,* 2d ed., 1988 revision (Chicago: American Library Association, 1988), 622 (hereafter cited as *AACR2R*).
2. *AACR2R,* 620.
3. *AACR2R,* 171.

Changes to Chapter 9

Edward Swanson

Most of the chapters in Parts I and II of the 1988 revision of AACR2 reflect, at most, a few major changes from the rules in the 1978 edition. Chapter 9, however, is essentially a completely new chapter.

When AACR2 was published in 1978, chapter 9 dealt exclusively with data files for mainframe computers, and the name of the chapter, "Machine-Readable Data Files," reflected this fact. Beginning in the early 1980s, microcomputer software, both data files and program files, became more prevalent. Librarians started to express dissatisfaction with the rules in chapter 9 for cataloging this software. Of major concern was the fact that, unlike the rest of AACR2, the rules for area 5 called for describing the contents of the item rather than the physical object itself, much as if one were to give the statement of extent of a sound recording in terms of the number of songs contained on it rather than describing it as one sound disc.

In January 1983, the ALA Committee on Cataloging: Description and Access (CC:DA) appointed a task force to examine the rules in chapter 9 to see how they might be applied to cataloging microcomputer software. The task force gave a preliminary report at the June 1983 meeting of CC:DA, and its final report was adopted at the January 1984 meeting of CC:DA. This report was published under the title *Guidelines for Using AACR2 Chapter 9 for Cataloging Microcomputer Software* (Chicago: American Library Association, 1984). The *Guidelines* were adopted by the Library of Congress and the major bibliographic utilities as an interim standard for use in cataloging microcomputer software in the United States.

As might be expected, the major difference between the 1978 edition of AACR2 and the *Guidelines* related to the physical description of the software. In the task force deliberations, proposals to retain the instructions in the 1978 edition for area 5 and to change area 5 to match the instructions for area 5 in the other chapters in Part I were debated heatedly. Pros and cons on both sides were discussed. Finally, CC:DA reached a compromise position. Area 5 would represent a combination of both the physical description of the carrier of the software and a description of the files contained within the software.

Other changes included expanding the instructions for area 2 for dealing with edition and edition-like statements found on microcomputer software (including the problem of determining what constitutes an edition statement) and the addition of a "System requirements" note in which to record information about the machine on which the software would run, information formerly included in area 5.

At its meeting in London in October 1986, the Joint Steering Committee for Revision of AACR completely revised chapter 9. The name of the chapter was changed from "Machine-Readable Data Files" to "Computer Files." The instructions were expanded to include all types of computer files, not just data files, and now also includes ones that are available to the user only by remote access.

This revised chapter was published jointly by the American Library Association, the Canadian Library Association, and the Library Association in 1987 under the title *Anglo-American Cataloguing Rules, Second Edition. Chapter 9, Computer Files, Draft Revision.*

Four major changes from the 1978 edition of AACR2 were made in this draft revision. The first was the change in the choice of chief source of information in rule 9.0B1. The 1978 edition gave preference to information found in an internal user label. If the information was not available in an internal user label, preference was given first to documentation issued by the creator, etc., of the file, next to other published descriptions of the file, and finally to other sources, including the container of the file and its labels.

The 1988 revision gives first preference to information found on title screens of the computer file. In cases where no title screen exists, the next preference is given to other internal information in a formal presentation, e.g., main menus or program statements. For items without internal information, the preference for the chief source of information is given first to information found on the physical carrier of the computer files (e.g., a floppy disk) and its labels. Next, preference is given to information found on the documentation issued by the publisher, etc., and finally to information printed on the container issued by the publisher, etc.

Rule 9.0B2 for prescribed sources of information for each of the areas of the description was changed to reflect the changes made in the choice of the chief source of information.

The second major change was the addition of area 3, the "file characteristics area." The area comprises first a designation of the type of file, using the terms "computer data," "computer program(s)," and "computer data and program(s)" (*see* figures 1–4).

This is followed by the number or approximate number of files that make up the content of the item (*see* figures 1–2). In addition to, or instead of, the number of files, other details also may be given. For computer data, these details are given in terms of the number or approximate number of records and/or bytes. For computer programs, these details are given in terms of the number or approximate number of statements and/or bytes. For files that include both data and programs, a combination of information is given. Essentially what was done with the creation of area 3 in chapter 9 was to provide an area in which to record much of the information formerly recorded in the specific material designation element of area 5 under the 1978 rules.

Each of the instructions in rules 9.3B1 and 9.3B2 is qualified with the phrase "readily available." This means that the cataloger does not have to search for this information to record an area 3, but rather transcribes information that is found in the normal course of cataloging the item. The rule also provides for omitting the numbering if it cannot be given succinctly. If such information is omitted from area 3, it may be given in a note according to the provisions of rule 9.7B8.

Perhaps the most major change in the revision of chapter 9 was the change made to area 5. As noted earlier, in the 1978 edition the rules called for recording information about the extent of the file(s) that made up the item. In the revised chapter 9, area 5 was changed to match area 5 in each of the other chapters in Part I of AACR2. In other words, the physical description area now describes the physical manifestation of the computer file. First the extent of the item is given, recording the number of physical units using arabic numerals and the appropriate specific material designation (*see* figures 1–4).

Rule 9.5C1 includes instructions for indicating the fact that the computer file is encoded to produce sound and/or to display in multiple colors (*see* figure 2). Optional rule 9.5C2 provides for recording physical characteristics such as the number of sides used, the recording density, and sectoring, if the information is readily available and is considered to

On title screen:

SIDEWAYS version 3.21
© Copyright 1982, 1985, 1987 Funk Software, Inc.

Directory   7 files
On container:

Version 3.2
Systems requirements: IBM PC, XT, AT, PS/2,
or compatibles, DOS version 2 or higher.
5 3/4" disk enclosed (may be exchanged for
3 1/2" format at no charge)

On manual title page:

SIDEWAYS

© Copyright 1985, 1987
Funk Software, Inc.
222 Hurd Street
Cambridge, MA 02142
(617) 497-6339

4th Edition
July, 1987

```
Sideways [computer file]. -- Version
3.21. -- Computer program (7 files). --
Cambridge, MA : Funk Software, c1987.
  1 computer disk ; 5 1/4 in. + 1 manual.

System requirements: IBM PC, XT, AT,
PS/2, or compatibles; DOS 2 or higher;
floppy disk or hard disk system.
  Title from title screen.
  Edition statement varies: Version 3.2
on container; version 3 on disk label.
  Edition statement on manual: 4th ed.
  Issued also on 3 1/2 in. computer
disk.
  Summary: A stand-alone formatting
program that rotates printouts 90
degrees on the page and writes across
perforations to give continuous output,
whatever the document width.  Works with
all programs that can print ASCII files.
```

Figure 1. Computer Disk

On title screen:

Lunar Greenhouse

MECC   Science
                                        Inquiry
                                        Collection

Copyright 1989

Disk label:

MECC   A-215

Lunar Greenhouse

Copyright MECC, 1989   Version 1.0

```
Lunar greenhouse [computer file]. --
Version 1.0. -- Computer program (2 files).
-- St. Paul, MN : MECC, 1989.
  1 computer disk : col. ; 5 1/4 cm. +
1 manual. -- (Science inquiry
collection)

  System requirements: Apple II series
computer with 128K RAM; color monitor
recommended; printer optional.
  Title from title screen.
  Intended audience: Grades 3-6, junior high
school.
  Summary: A discovery-learning
simulation that allows students to test
how each of four variables influences
how well a vegetable plant grows and
produces vegetables ...
  "A-215."
  ISBN 0-87490-703-9.
```

Figure 2.   Computer Disk

be important. The 1978 edition of AACR2 provided for recording such information in a note.

Rule 9.5D was added to provide for recording the dimensions of the physical carrier (*see* figures 1–4). Rule 9.5E was simplified basically to an instruction to follow the instructions in rule 1.5E for recording information about accompanying material (*see* figures 1–4).

For files that are available only by remote access, however, area 4 is omitted (*see* figure 5).

On disk 1:

| | GRATEFUL
MED | Master MeSH (1989) Disk - Version 4.0
National Library of Medicine |

On disk 2:

| | GRATEFUL
MED | Master Program Disk - Version 4.0
National Library of Medicine |

On manual title page:

GRATEFUL MED

User's Guide
Version 4.0

U.S. DEPARTMENT OF
HEALTH AND HUMAN SERVICES
National Institutes of Health
National Library of Medicine

```
Grateful med [computer file]. -- Version
4.0. -- Computer program. -- [Bethesda, Md.]
: National Library of Medicine, [1989].
   2 computer disks ; 5 1/4 in. + 1 user's
guide.

   System requirements: IBM PC family or
fully compatible; DOS version 2.0 or
higher; Hayes Smartmodem or fully
compatible modem; 256K RAM or more; 1
360K double-sided, double-density
diskette drive; 1.5MB on a hard disk
optional.
   Title from disk label.
   Summary: A software tool designed to
simplify the process of searching the
National Library of Medicine's Medical
Literature Analysis and Retrieval System
(MEDLARS).
   Contents: Master program disk --
Master MeSH (1989) disk.
```

Figure 3. Computer Disk

The last major change made to chapter 9 was the addition of a new note called the "System requirements" note. This is given as the first note and includes some information that formerly was included in the physical description area. It includes, in this order, information on the make and

On disk:

Disk Technician Advanced   Version 3   Rev. 5.20
Serial # 2708-0727-34

Automated AI Software System   Prime Solutions

On manual title page:

Disk Technician Advanced

Automated AI Software System

User's Manual
Version Number DTM09308

Prime Solutions Incorporated

```
Disk technician advanced [computer file]
: automated AI software system. --
Version 3, rev. 5.20. -- Computer
program. -- San Diego, CA : Prime
Solutions, Inc., 1988.
    1 computer disk ; 5 1/4 in. + 1
user's manual.

    System requirements: IBM PC, XT, AT,
derivative, or true hardware/software
BIOS compatible IBM clone; PC or MS-DOS
version 2.1 to 3.32; 512K of RAM.
    Title from disk label.
    User's manual has version number:
DTM09308.
    Also issued as 3 1/2 in. disk.
    Summary: ...
    "Serial# 2708-0727-34."
```

Figure 4.   Computer Disk

model of the computer(s) on which the file is designed to run; the amount of memory required to run the program; the name of the operating system used; any software requirements, including the programming languages; and, the kind and characteristics of any required or recommended peripherals (*see* figures 1–4). As is true in area 3, the instruction is qualified by the phrase "readily available."

For remote access files, the system requirements note is replaced by a note giving the mode of access. Unlike the system requirements note, however, this note is required (*see* figure 5).

```
OCLC online union catalog [computer file].
-- Computer data. -- Dublin, Ohio : OCLC,
1972-

Mode of access: Direct access terminal to
OCLC, dial access, or through the EPIC
Service.  System available Monday-Friday,
6:00 a.m. to 10:00 p.m., E.T., and Saturday,
8:00 a.m. to 8:00 p.m., E.T.
Title from accompanying documentation.
Summary: Contains more that 24 million
bibliographic records for works dating from
approximately 2150 B.C. to the present in
all types of formats and in more than 300
languages.  Includes holdings information for
over 9,000 member institutions in 26
countries.
```

Figure 5. Remote Access Computer File

Other changes to chapter 9 are less major, but nevertheless important. Rule 9.1B1 was changed to a reference to the instructions in rule 1.1B. Although not specified in rule 9.1C1, the general material designation used for computer files in rule 1.1C was changed from "machine-readable data file" to "computer file" (*see* figures 1–5).

Rule 9.7B2, the note relating to language and script, was limited to the language(s) and/or script(s) of the written or spoken contents of the file. Programming languages, formerly recorded in this note, now are recorded in the system requirements note.

Rule 9.7B3 was changed to require that the source of the title proper always be given (*see* figures 1–5). This also is reflected in the addition of rule 9.1B2, which gives the same instruction, as opposed to the instruction in rule 9.1B1 in the 1978 edition that required such a note only in the case when the title had been taken from outside the file itself.

The rule for edition and history, rule 9.7B7, was changed to require that the source of an edition statement always be given if it is different from the source of the title proper. Rule 9.7B8 was changed from a rule for recording program version and/or level to one for giving important file characteristics that have not been recorded in area 3 already. In addition, it is used for recording extensive numbering that cannot be recorded in area 3 succinctly.

Rule 9.7B10 limits the physical descripion note to important physical details that are not recorded in area 5, particularly if they affect the use of the item. Physical characteristics of remote access files also are recorded in this note, subsuming information formerly recorded in the mode of use note (rule 9.7B15 in the 1978 edition).

Rule 9.7B14 now is limited to a note on the intended audience for, or the intellectual level of, a computer file (*see* figure 2). Rule 9.7B16 was expanded to include other machine-readable versions of the computer file, rather than being limited to other formats in which the data content of the file was available as was true in the 1978 edition. This other formats note now reflects the change made throughout Part I of AACR2 for recording general information about other formats in which an item is available, whether those other formats are in the cataloging agency or not (*see* figure 4).

The provision for recording the number of logical records or statements for each part of a file named in a contents note was dropped from rule 9.7B18. The scope of rule 9.7B20 was expanded to include restrictions on use of a computer file, formerly included in rule 9.7B14. The rule itself was changed basically to a reference to the instructions in rule 1.7B20. In addition, instructions for recording a locally assigned file or data set name, and for giving the date when the content of the file was copied from, or transferred to, another source were added.

Rule 9.7B21 dealing with "with" notes was added in keeping with the rules for notes in other chapters of Part I.

Changes to Part II, Headings, Uniform Titles, and References

Carlen Ruschoff

The revisions in Part II of the 1988 revision of the *Anglo-American Cataloguing Rules* (AACR2R) fall into four general categories. The first is one in which minor errors have been corrected in the original text. It needs little comment here. The second category involves the rearrangement of the order in which rules appear to make the sequence of rules reflect the sequence of steps in the cataloger's decision-making process. The third group of changes provides more specific guidelines in ambiguous cases with an eye to simplifying application, standardizing practice, and improving consistency in the formulation of headings. The final and most important set involves substantial changes to the instructions to the cataloger. These revisions are significant not only because they result in a change in cataloging practice but also because they result in a heading that makes more sense to the catalog user. Examples of each of these types of revisions are given and discussed in the following paragraphs. The article concludes with a list of the major changes in Part II of AACR2R.

For those interested in changes of the first type, which are primarily typographic corrections, the most exhaustive source is Edward Swanson's *Changes to the* Anglo-American Cataloguing Rules, *Second Edition* (Soldier Creek Press, 1989), which details every change from the most minor to the most comprehensive.

Changes of the second type, rearrangement of rules for ease of use, are welcome to catalogers. The most extensive reorganization of rules is found in chapter 25 in the rules for formulating uniform titles for musical works, rules 25.25–25.35. The rules were reorganized to replicate the series of decisions a cataloger must make to formulate a uniform title. In their revised form, the rules break down the title into units and lead the cataloger through the construction of the title, step by step.

An example of another sort of rule reorganization can be found in chapter 22 under the rules providing for additions to names. In this case, rules were regrouped so that they appear in a more logical sequence. The provisions listed for additions to names entered under given name, etc., were moved from old rule 22.17 to rule 22.16, and the substance of old rule 22.16, additions to names consisting of or containing initials, was incorporated into the suite of rules providing for additions to identical names. This realignment resulted in a more sensible and useful grouping of instructions for additions to identical names.

Changes of the third type are more significant. These provide specific guidance to catalogers facing ambiguous cases by removing ambiguity, streamlining the decision tree, and simplifying the process so that they are able to create consistent headings quickly. By giving more direction to the cataloger, the time-consuming portions of the decision-making process, especially the interpretation of rule application and the verification process, are removed. Many of the rules revised between 1978 and 1988 fall into this category. Of these, most were changed only slightly, but some were extensively reworked.

One example of those extensively reworked is rule 21.2, which provides direction on when the title of a work has changed. This rule was recast from the positive to the negative, in the sense that in the earlier edition, instruction was given on when to consider a title changed. In the new edition, however, a briefer instruction is given, followed by a list of common variations in titles that do not amount to a title change.

Another example of rule clarification comes into play in the case where names of bodies or government agencies that may be entered subordinately are described. Rules 24.13 and 24.18 list "types" of names that are always entered subordinate to a higher body. In the 1978 edition, type 3 was intended to provide direction for entering a name that is likely to be used by another body. Names like "Research Institute" and "Centre de documentation" are indistinct headings since many different organizations are likely to have research institutes or centres de documentation. The old rule required that there be a conflict with another body or agency name for subordinate entry to be considered. The rewritten rule simply declares that names of a general nature are entered subordinately to a higher body. The qualification of conflict was removed from the instruction to make the catalogers's decision process easier and quicker to execute.

To specify further the instances when a body or agency is entered subordinately, a new "type" was added to rules 24.13 and 24.18. Some names encountered by catalogers do not convey the idea of being a corporate body. There were no explicit instructions for entering names of bodies or agencies such as "Collection Development" or "Research and Analysis" in AACR2. This new provision for subordinate bodies was inserted in both rules as type 4.

The fourth category of revision made to AACR2 between 1978 and 1988 involves those revisions that result in a change in cataloging practice. These changes have an impact on the bibliographic records in the catalog since they result in a change in choice of entry or form of entry. The two most significant examples of this type of change include the rules for entry under pseudonyms, and entry of places in the British Isles.

The rules for entry under pseudonyms were completely recast to allow the cataloger to use multiple name headings for authors who write under more than one name. Two new rules were added to the section on pseudonyms in chapter 22 to provide guidance. Rule 22.2B2 was added to provide for authors who have more than one "bibliographic identity," that is, the author clearly uses a distinct name for each group of works he or she produces. The new rule instructs the cataloger to enter groups of works under the name that is identified with that group and to make references to connect the names. For example, Charles L. Dodgson used his real name for works on mathematics and logic; however, he used the pseudonym Lewis Carroll in his literary works. Under the new rule 22.2B2 for authors having separate bibliographic identities, the cataloger enters all his works on mathematics and logic under the heading for Dodgson and all of his literary works under the heading for Carroll.

The other rule added to this section, 22.2B3, applies to contemporary authors who use more than one name in their works, whether pseudonyms or their real names. The new rule directs the cataloger to enter a work by a contemporary author under the name that appears in the work and to make references connecting the names used by the author. The addition of this rule and the change in cataloging practice have two benefits. Not only do they simplify the decision regarding choice of name by relieving the cataloger of the time-consuming task of determining whether the author has a predominate name, but they also produce catalog headings that are likely to be familiar to the catalog user.

Another example of the change-in-practice category concerns revisions to the rules for formulating headings for places in the British Isles, rule 23.4D. The rules in the 1978 text directed the cataloger to qualify a place in the United Kingdom, other than a county or a place within a city, by the appropriate county name or island name. This rule was difficult for catalogers unfamiliar with place names in the United Kingdom to apply since it required familiarity with the British county structure. Catalogers working in large libraries within the United Kingdom also reportedly found the rule impossible to apply, since it required overwhelming changes in existing catalog files.

Under the revised rule, place names in the British Isles are qualified by the appropriate jurisdiction: England, Ireland, Northern Ireland, Scotland, Wales, Isle of Man, or Channel Islands. Examples of changes in headings resulting from this revision include:

```
1978    Oxford (Oxfordshire)
1988    Oxford (England)

1978    Edinburgh (Lothian)
1988    Edinburgh (Scotland)

1978    Ballybunion (Kerry)
1988    Ballybunion (Ireland)
```

These are only a few examples of each of the four types of revisions found in Part II of AACR2R, but collectively they give a sense of the changes made. The remainder of this article lists the major changes made to Part II between 1978 and 1988.

Chapter 21. Choice of Access Points

21.1A. Works of Personal Authorship

The definition of works of personal authorship was broadened in the revised edition. The examples of types of personal authors that appeared in AACR2 were deleted and a reference to subsequent rules in the chapter for specific applications took their place.

21.1B. Entry under Corporate Body

Rule 21.1B2 was expanded to include three additional categories of works that qualify for entry under a corporate body:

1. Religious laws and liturgical works were incorporated into category
   (b), which was formerly limited to legal and governmental works.
2. Works that are written records of performances were added to category (e), which provides for works that result from the collective
   activity of a performing group. (A written record of performance is
   a publication that is created after the performers record a performance.)
3. Category (f) was added to include cartographic materials that
   emanate from a corporate body.

21.2. Changes in Titles Proper

The definition of a change in title proper outlined in rule 21.2A was rewritten
to provide more direction to the cataloger. Specific conditions under which
a title is not considered to have changed were added to this rule. The recast
rule conforms with current ISBD(S) guidelines.

Four conditions are listed; only three of them are new criteria. The first
states that a title has not changed if the representation of a word or words is
changed. Three examples of word representation are included: abbreviated
word or symbol vs. spelled-out form, singular vs. plural form, and one
spelling vs. another. Each of the following conditions is *not* considered a
title change:

1. abbreviated word or symbol vs. spelled-out form

```
The Bowker Annual of Library and Book Trade
   Information, 1971

The Bowker Annual of Library & Book Trade
   Information, 1972
```

2. singular vs. plural form

```
Sciences & Technologies

Science & Technologie
```

3. one spelling vs. another

```
Centralblatt für Bakteriologie,
   Parasitenkunde, und Infektionskrankheiten

Zentralblatt für Bakteriologie,
   Parasitenkunde, und Infektionskrankheiten
```

Another circumstance where the cataloger is instructed not to consider the title to have changed is when the only change is the addition or deletion of the name of the issuing body at the *end* of the title. For example:

```
Transactions

Transactions of the Royal Society of
    Edinburgh
```

A third guideline added to this rule directs the cataloger not to consider a title to have changed when the only change is in punctuation.

21.6. Works of Shared Responsibility
21.6C. Principal Responsibility Not Indicated

A new paragraph was added in rule 21.6C1 to give instruction on how to handle cases in which the names of persons or bodies appear in a different order on the chief sources of information of different editions of a work. The cataloger is instructed to enter each edition under the heading for the person or body named first in that edition. For example:

```
    International marketing / by John M. Hess
    and Philip R. Cateora. -- Homewood, Ill. :
    Irwin, 1966.
    Main entry under the heading for John M.
    Hess
    Added entry under the heading for Philip R.
    Cateora

    International marketing / by Philip R.
    Cateora and John M. Hess. -- Rev. ed. --
    Homewood, Ill. : Irwin, 1971.
    Main entry under the heading for Philip
    R. Cateora
    Added entry under the heading for John
    M. Hess
```

21.12. Revisions of Texts

The rules in this section have been reworked to simplify the choice of entry for a work that has been revised by a person or body other than the original author of the text. The provisions for headings for "revisions of texts" in

AACR2 required research and judgment on the part of the cataloger to determine whether to enter the work under the heading for the original author or the revisor. The choice often resulted in a main entry heading that made little sense to library users. In AACR2R, the criteria under which the choice of entry is made are more specific, leaving less room for the cataloger's judgment and requiring no background research. The conditions under which the original author is considered responsible for a revised work now are more restrictive. The original author is considered responsible for a revision in only two cases: (1) the original author is named in the statement of responsibility, or, (2) the original author is named in the title proper and no other person is named in a statement of responsibility or other title information. If, however, the chief source of information indicates that a person or body other than the original author is responsible for the item being cataloged, the work is entered under the heading for the reviser. The application of the revised rules results in a different choice of entry for some works. For example:

```
Immroth's guide to the Library of Congress
    classification / by Lois Mai Chan. --
    3rd ed.
```

Under AACR2, the main entry is under the heading for Immroth. According to the rules in AACR2R, the main entry is under the heading for Chan.

21.23. Sound Recordings
21.23D. Works by Different Persons or Bodies

Rules 21.23C–D were recast to provide music-based criteria for entering sound recordings of works by different persons or bodies. The rules in AACR2 directed that works by different persons or bodies were to be entered under the heading for the principal performer. This instruction resulted in confusing entries in which the principal performer appears to be responsible for a work composed by another person or body. The revised rules rectify this problem by providing criteria that direct the cataloger to enter works under the heading for the principal performer when the work has a collective title (usually works that feature a performance) and when the participation of the performer(s) goes beyond mere performance (works of popular, rock, and jazz music). When the work is a recording of "serious" nature, such as classical music, the cataloger is directed to enter the work under the heading for the composer.

Chapter 22. Headings for Persons

22.1. General Rule for Choice of Name

An instruction was added to rule 22.1A to specify the treatment of roman numerals associated with a given name. These numerals are to be treated as part of the name.

22.2.B. Choice among Different Names. Pseudonyms

The rules for entering a work under a pseudonym were completely recast both to simplify the choice of name entry and to provide access points that would seem logical to catalog users. Two new ideas were introduced into this suite of rules. The first is the concept of bibliographic identity (e.g., an author who uses different names for different types of works). The second is the practice of using the name that appears on the chief source of information for a contemporary author even though the author may have other, more predominant names.

22.8. Entry under Given Name, Etc. Names of Royal Persons

Provisions for royal persons were added to this suite of rules as rule 22.8C1.

22.11. Entry under Phrase

Rules 22.11A–B were rewritten to encompass forenames that are preceded by words other than a term of address or a title of position or office, e.g., Boy George.

22.16. Additions to Names Entered under Given Name, Etc.

Rules 22.16–22.18 were rearranged to group additions to specific types of names together. AACR2R groups additions to given names under rule 22.16 and additions to distinguish identical names in rules 22.17–22.19.

22.16A3. Consorts of Royal Persons (Old Rule 22.17A4)

The rule was revised to allow catalogers to add to the heading of consorts of royal persons who are known by their own titles (e.g., Eleanor of

Aquitaine). This rule was revised to allow the addition of the consort's title
to the heading.

```
1978    Eleanor, Queen consort of Henry II,
   King of England

1988    Eleanor, of Aquitaine, Queen,
   consort of Henry II, King of England
```

Chapter 23. Geographic names

23.4. Additions to Geographic Names

The general rule providing guidance for adding a qualifier to geographic
names has been rewritten to incorporate the first option from AACR2 into
the instruction. The new rule instructs the cataloger to qualify a place name
by the name of a larger jurisdiction. The rule no longer provides options to
the cataloger.

23.4C. Places in Australia, Canada, Malaysia, United States, U.S.S.R., or Yugoslavia

This rule was expanded to include places in Malaysia, U.S.S.R., and Yugo-
slavia, and the special rule for places in Malaysia, the U.S.S.R., or Yugo-
slavia (old rule 23.4E) was deleted. Rule 23.4C1 was added to give the
specific instruction that the country qualifier is not added to headings for
states, provinces, territories, etc., within the countries listed above.

23.4D. Places in the British Isles

The rules guiding the additions to place names in the British Isles were
completely recast making their application simpler.

The first rule in this section, rule 23.4D1, lists the places in the British
Isles that do not require a qualifier. They are England, the Republic of
Ireland, Northern Ireland, Scotland, Wales, the Isle of Man, and the Channel
Islands.

Rule 23.4D2 was revised to direct the cataloger to qualify places in
England, the Republic of Ireland, Northern Ireland, Scotland, Wales, the Isle
of Man, and the Channel Islands by the appropriate country name, e.g.,
Glasgow (Scotland). The corresponding rule in AACR2 instructed the
cataloger to add the name of the county.

Chapter 24. Headings for Corporate Bodies

24.4. Additions to Headings When Two or More Bodies Have the Same or Similar Names

The rule change deleted the option to make additions to headings even if there is no need to distinguish between bodies. A new sentence was added allowing the cataloger to add a qualifier to a corporate body if it "assists in the understanding of the nature or purpose of the body."

24.5A. Omissions from Corporate Name Headings

Rule 24.5A1 was revised to direct the cataloger to omit an initial article unless the heading is to be filed under the article.

24.13 and 24.18. Entry of Subordinate Bodies and Government Agencies, Types 3 and 4

The type 3 category in AACR2 encompassed names that are likely to be used by more than one higher body. The cataloger was instructed to enter names subordinately only when they were in conflict with a name used by another agency. For example, "Statistics and Data Research Office" is an example of a name that might be used by other bodies. The rule was rewritten to remove the criterion for conflict and to instruct the cataloger simply to enter subordinately a name that is of a "general nature or does no more than indicate a geographic, chronological, or numbered or lettered subdivision" of a parent body or government agency.

Type 4 was added to both of these rules to provide instruction on creating headings for bodies whose names do not convey the idea of being a corporate body, e.g., "Human Development and Relations."

Chapter 25. Uniform Titles

25.2A. General Rule

The rule in AACR2 directed the cataloger to use a uniform title only in two situations: (1) when the title proper of a work differs from the uniform title; or, (2) when the addition of another element is required to organize the file. In AACR2R, the first condition has been rewritten to make the statement clearer. The second condition remains unchanged, but provisions 3 and 4 are new. They are: provision 3, when the title used as the main or added entry heading for a work needs to be distinguished from that of a different work; and, provision 4, when the title of the work is obscured by introductory words or statements of responsibility.

25.2C1. Initial Articles

An instruction to omit an initial article from a uniform title was added.

25.25–25.35. Musical Works

The rules for formulating a uniform title for a musical work were reorganized to replicate the cataloger's decision-making process.

25.26A and 25.28

The general rule introduces the concept of "initial title element," on which the uniform title for a musical work is constructed. Complete instructions on how to isolate the initial title element are given in rule 25.28.

After AACR2R: The Future of the *Anglo-American Cataloguing Rules*

Michael Gorman

The year 1968, a year not without significance for the nation and the world, was an important year for librarianship and for bibliographic control. It signified three of many things and the beginning of the Modern Age of cataloguing and the use of catalogues. Marc II, OCLC, and the first editions (British and American) of the *Anglo-American Cataloguing Rules* (AACR) all became part of the collective cataloguing consciousness in that fateful year. Their subsequent interconnections and the influence of other developments, other standards, and other institutions have combined to create the complex, rich, and sometimes difficult to understand environment in which we now practice the profession of librarianship and, in particular, the craft of cataloguing.

In 1978, the second edition of AACR (AACR2) was published. Its creation and publication were attended by misplaced hysteria and a crass "know-nothingism" that delayed its implementation for two years. In the meantime, the MARC juggernaut continued to roll, and the number of MARC records in the world grew into the millions (by now, the tens of millions). I would estimate that the delay in implementing AACR2 was the cause of the addition of at least half a million MARC records that have had, subsequently, to be upgraded.

Now, in 1988, we have the publication of the first full-scale revision of AACR2 (now becoming known as AACR2R). If things stay on the same timetable, we can expect 1998 to see the publication of another revision (AACR2R2? AACR3?). I shall try here to peer into the future and to see

what the end of the millennium holds for descriptive cataloguing in particular and cataloguing in general.

In order to predict the future one must understand the context of the
present and extrapolate that context into the likely future. There are so many
things that have changed utterly since 1968, there are so many differences
between the cataloguing experience then and the cataloguing experience
now, that it is sometimes difficult to see the present context clearly and
perilous to guess what the future holds.

We know that the advent of online bibliographic control systems (invari-
ably, but mistakenly, called "online catalogues") and the rise of the bibliographic networks (most notably and influentially, OCLC) have had an
enormous impact on the way in which we think about and practice cataloguing. We also know that the creation of second generation online bibliographic control systems and changes in the practices and role of the networks
have the potential to change cataloguing even more.

What we do not know, and can only guess, is the impact of emerging
technologies and, for example, expert systems, on the nature and practice
of cataloguing. It is more than likely, however, that standardized and
formalized bibliographic records of one kind or another will be a necessary
part of any foreseeable bibliographic control systems. Proponents of the
"paperless society" (which, as I understand it, is a concept that predicts the
demise of all library materials and their replacement by electronic communication) would, presumably, argue that bibliographic control would be
unnecessary in their counter-Utopia. History will judge them right or wrong.

There are also those who advocate the transfer of printed and other texts
into "full text" systems in which the entire texts would be searchable and,
hence, formalized records of those texts would be otiose. Since this proposition is espoused by, among others, one of my heroes—Fred Kilgour—I am
hesitant to be negative about it. Still, I cannot see how such a system of any
size would prevent the creation of enough "noise" to deafen the entire
population of, say, Columbus, Ohio.

If we are to go on creating and using formalized bibliographic records,
the major structure within which we have to work is that of the MARC
formats. If there is to be a new age of cataloguing that includes any radical
revision of AACR, there will have to be substantial and positive changes
made to those formats. In order to understand this last, we have to go back
to the origin and history of MARC.

Contrary to what revisionist historians have had to say, the fact is that
MARC was modelled on the catalogue card. To all intents and purposes, it

is an electronic catalogue card. This harsh judgement is based not only on the fact that the fields and subfields of MARC follow the order and analysis of data of the catalogue card, it is also based on the very nature of the MARC record. The catalogue card is a unitary record for a physical object (or set of physical objects) containing complex bibliographic data of various kinds.

Exactly the same description applies to the MARC record. Those unitary records (cards and MARC) have few links to other records—far fewer than the actual complexities of the relationships between physical objects and the works that they represent demand. Even the correspondence of the fields and subfields of MARC to the structure of the catalogue card has had more than a cosmetic impact. Most notoriously, there can be little doubt that the fact that a MARC record demands a 1XX field has been the main reason that, in the fading years of the twentieth century, cataloguers and cataloguing codes are still concerned with the question of "main entry"—an archaic irrelevance rooted in the printed book catalogue.

It is evident to me that, if cataloguing rules (and other bibliographic standards) are to evolve to a higher plane, it is essential that the MARC format be reevaluated and radically recast. In terms of *Realpolitik,* it is hard to see such a major change being achieved. One has only to think of the many millions of MARC records already in existence and the multitude of programs and systems that are based on the MARC-record-as-it-is to realize that progress on this front would be very hard won. On the other hand, the stultifying effect of those records and systems will only increase with time, and change will become ever more difficult as the weary world turns.

Ever the Pollyanna, I shall assume for the purposes of argument, that our profession is willing to entertain the thought of drastic change to achieve beneficial aims and that the MARC system will be revamped to suit the needs of advanced bibliographic control systems. In essence, that change would consist of replacing the unitary MARC record containing complex information and with few and weak links to other related unitary records. Its replacement (MARC III? HYPERMARC?) would be a system based on multiple records for each physical object, set of physical objects, intellectually distinct part of a physical object, and work. Those records would contain simple data and would be linked in an articulated, complex, and sophisticated manner. An individual record would contain (for example):

a description, including coded data (the description could be of an
    object, part of an object, or a set of objects); or
name authority data; or
uniform title authority data; or

subject access data (the data could be a package containing, for example, a DC number, LC subject heading(s), PRECIS string, or an individual subject authority record).

The elegance and flexibility of the system would reside in the various ways of linking these records to create a complex structure expressive of all the bibliographic relationships between works and objects (e.g., between the work expressed as **Carroll, Lewis. Alice in Wonderland** and a particular manifestation of that work), between works and other works (e.g., between the work expressed as **Dickens, Charles. Oliver Twist** and the work expressed as **Bart, Lionel. Oliver!**); between a bibliographic description and the subject authorities that pertain to the work of which the object described is a manifestation; and between related bibliographic descriptions (e.g., for a series, a publication within a series, and analytical descriptions of parts of that publication).

If MARC were to be changed so drastically, the way would be open for a radical recasting of the *Anglo-American Cataloguing Rules,* one that would go well beyond mere revising of AACR2. The result would not, in my opinion, be AACR3. It would be something that would more appropriately be called *The HYPERMARC Record Preparation Manual—Bibliographic* (a complement to *The HYPERMARC Record Preparation Manual—Subjects).* What would such a manual contain? It would, like AACR2, have two parts and those parts would relate to (1) description, and (2) access; however, the content and internal organization of the parts would be, in some cases, very different.

Part 1 of the manual would still be based on the twin concepts of ISBD and the elaborating of a preceding general chapter in later chapters dealing with specific kinds of library material. Fundamentally, therefore, the Part 1 of the proposed new manual would be similar to that of Part I of AACR2. However, there would be three important differences. First, there would be instructions on how to assign HYPERMARC designations ("tags" and "codes") to the descriptive data that are being recorded. Second, there would be rules for the assignment of fixed-length field codes, etc., that are of a descriptive nature. Third, and most significantly, there would be a much more thorough working out of the rules for analysis and rules on when analytical entries should be made.

One of the great barriers to standardization in modern cataloguing is the persistent reluctance of cataloguing rules to prescribe the focus of the bibliographic description. To take the most obvious example, the cataloguer is nowhere instructed on the question of whether to catalogue a set as a set or to catalogue the individual items separately. Since every library has its own (often internally inconsistent) policy, the resulting records render the use of the network database a matter, very often, of chance. In the revision of MARC that I envisage, this question would be less important, since full records would exist at each "level" of description. Thus, retrieval of descriptive data would be equally possible at, say, the series, monograph, and analytical "levels." The new manual would prescribe the "levels" at which description is to be done and the ways in which those descriptions are to be linked. Thus the resulting cluster of records in the database would be neutral in that the library using the cluster could choose the level of focus, if one were deemed necessary.

Part 2 of the proposed new manual would be, in essence, a set of rules on the construction of name, title, and name/title authority packages (i.e., authority records plus); on the linkage of the packages to bibliographic descriptions and to other packages; and on the assignment of fixed length field and other MARC codes of importance for access. To take the simplest example, the present chapter on geographic names (chapter 23) would be replaced by a set of rules on the assembling of a name access package to denote each place; how to choose the "preferred form" from among variant names for the same place (though access by any of the variant forms would be as effective as access by the "preferred" form); how and when to assign geographic area codes (from a list contained in the chapter); and how to tag and code all these data.

Since HYPERMARC will recognize the inutility of the main entry concept, there will be no need for the present chapter 21. In its place, there will be a general chapter on the links that are to be made between descriptions and access packages. The specific chapters will make reference to those links, but the replacement for chapter 21 will survey and exemplify the whole concept. Logically, it should follow (rather than precede) the chapters on personal, geographic, and corporate names and the chapter on uniform titles. In sum, the new Part 2 will consist of five chapters—the first four dealing with the construction of different kinds of names and title access packages and the last dealing with the ways in which those packages and descriptive records are linked to create complex clusters of bibliographic information. It should be noted that not only will the distinction between main and added entries vanish, but also the distinction between "headings" and "references" will be diminished and, in many applications, will vanish altogether.

Supposing all of the foregoing does not come to pass and we remain in the iron grip of an outdated technology expressed in the MARC system, what then? The answer is that there will never be an AACR3 or, even better, a code that replaces and moves beyond the AACR idea. This does not mean that there is no necessity, in the absence of a complete overhaul of MARC, for revisions of AACR2. If the new publication is AACR2.5, we will need an AACR2.75, etc. Such future revisions will, like the youngest sons in fairy tales, have three tasks.

First, to get rid of the detritus that AACR2 and AACR2R still carry from previous codes. The most obnoxious of these (the rule in appendix A that dictates that the first word following an article in a title "main entry" is to be capitalized—a piece of nonsense that should have died before Hitler's war) is merely the best known of a number of hangovers from the past that need to be removed. Second, there is the absurd elaboration of rules dealing with (to cite the worst examples) legal materials, music uniform titles, and the Bible. Lubetzky fought the good fight and his ideas about codes based on principle rather than legalism ("case law") have, to a great extent, been embodied in the AACR editions. The kind of creeping legalism that the elaborations mentioned above exemplify should be rooted out. Their substance could, if necessary, be contained in manuals for specialist cataloguers. In addition, the ethnocentrism implied in the rules for the Bible has no part in AACR, which is, to a very great extent, already a world code. The third task will be to accommodate changes brought about by new technologies in future revisions.

It seems to me that AACR2R is the best code of descriptive cataloguing that we have or can have, given the politico-bibliographic climate and the stultifying effect of the MARC format and the systems that are based upon it. Any genuine advance beyond this point will demand attitudinal changes (are we cataloguers and lapsed cataloguers prepared to be progressive and even radical in our approach? I think so) and changes in the context in which cataloguing is carried out (are library administrators, the LC/OCLC/RLIN complex, and the vendors of systems prepared to be progressive and even radical in their approach? I sincerely doubt it). In the absence of such changes we will have a good descriptive cataloguing code for the early machine age (the age that is passing) but, alas, one that will not wear well as time progresses and technology advances. *Aux armes, citoyens!* The time for a new bibliographic revolution is now.

Does Cataloging Theory Rest on a Mistake?

Michael Carpenter

In his "After AACR2R: The Future of the *Anglo-American Cataloguing Rules*," Michael Gorman presents a vision of a code for the preparation of entries for a truly online cataloging code that is at once compelling and only slightly different from views he has presented as long ago as 1977.[1] Given that his vision of an online catalog seems so straightforward yet so old, why is it that no working exemplar yet exists? Until such a catalog exists, of course, the kind of code Gorman discusses will not be written.

In the compilation of a set of catalog rules, two considerations come into play, the technological and the conceptual. Technological considerations include the ease with which a catalog can display bibliographical information in varying fashions. Although there is no "logical" reason such changes in presentations cannot be done with a catalog using more or less permanent displays of information, such as cards, COMfiche, bookform catalogs, etc., it is intuitively clear that construction of such a catalog in the forms just described would involve a very large number of entries, far in excess of what we have in the modern card catalog. There would be a complete set of listings of an author's works under each form of the author's name. There would be multiple displays under each form of the title of a work that had appeared with various titles. Such a catalog would obviate the need for references at a high price in space; in fact, it is precisely to avoid such situations that references were developed in the first place. The vast majority of online catalogs today have fixed displays, much as did the paper catalogs of old. Catalogs with fixed form displays seem, at first blush, to call for a different sort of theory than do catalogs with more easily changed forms of displays.

If catalogs with fixed forms of display determine the type of cataloging theory that is used, then cataloging theory as we know it now rests on a mistake, the mistake of established, immutable, uniform headings. One of the questions probed here is whether this mistake will affect the nature of the objectives of a catalog instead of just the means by which we achieve them. Cataloging theory is conceptual in nature and should not be confused with questions about the way in which we transcribe cataloging data or the correct form of heading for a certain class of individuals or bodies.

To examine the question, we need to examine what happens in a hypothetical computer catalog using CRT displays only; to do so will provide a certain amount of visualization of the questions under discussion. I will define it as a catalog in which manipulations of the data in the base can be performed virtually at will. I must also stress that there appears to be no working exemplar of a catalog using files of a size likely to be of interest in a large library. For example, the capability to make changes on a real-time basis on the headings preceding a bibliographical description does not exist at the moment for such a setting. Furthermore, the changes must be transitory, affecting the display only.

As Gorman points out, the establishment of a single "official" form of name is meaningless in an online catalog; there is no requirement that the number of entries, main and added, be limited to only one for each person or body associated with the work in order that space needed for the catalog not become much too bulky. In fixed-form catalogs, establishment of "official" forms of name has been required in order to keep growth of the catalog within bounds. To apply older subject cataloging terminology to author-title cataloging, it was necessary to suppress synonyms. To define what a synonym was in terms of personal and corporate names became a whole branch of cataloging theory; we had to have a procedure for deciding when a group of people became a new corporate body, when a person established new "bibliographic identities," etc. Here is one place where traditional cataloging theory has been based on a mistake; the metaphor of a fixed-form display caused a whole branch of theory to form. It was a necessary mistake; fixed-form displays require a uniform heading to work easily.

In modern times the mistake was beatified in the "Statement of Principles" adopted at the 1961 International Conference on Cataloguing Principles in Paris. The statement speaks constantly of the need for uniform headings, by which is meant "one particular form of the author's name or one particular title, or, for books not identified by author or title, a uniform heading consisting of a suitable substitute for the title."[2]

The mistake was canonized in the separation between the MARC authority and bibliographic formats, with two disadvantages. The first was the severing of the logical relation between headings for bibliographic records and the data for establishing their form in a particular fashion. The second was that the isolation of the established form from new bibliographic records permitted inconsistent headings to enter the national database; the fact that (say) Huey Long's name is to be found in three different forms in the OCLC database, with the consequent difficulty of finding material by Long, is a legacy of this separation of authority and bibliographic records.

Of the two disadvantages of severing the authority and bibliographic formats, the first, that of losing the logical relationship, has probably done the more long-term damage. The second disadvantage, that of allowing non-uniform headings to enter a database constructed on the basis of uniform headings, can be cleaned up with sufficient labor. The first, however, prevents the construction of a true online catalog of the sort envisioned by Gorman. Although the mistake is understandable—fixed-form displays, even on computers, were essentially the only available models at the time of the Paris conference and the beginnings of MARC—it has had the consequences mentioned above.

To correct the mistake and adapt cataloging theory to a true online environment, we must revise our terminology slightly. For example, instead of discussing references to a fixed form of name, we shall talk about links among the various forms of name.[3] A name may stand for the name of a corporate body, a person, or a work. With this slight revision we can engage on the hypothetical outlining of a code to replace current chapters relating to form and choice of heading.

With reference to corporate names, problems relating to subordination would no longer exist. Links might be established to cover searches so precise that publications of a particular subordinate body are desired only if a particular superior body was controlling the subordinate body at the time of publication. Aside from wishes commonly expressed by government documents librarians, I doubt such a precise search would ever be necessary. Yet the capability could exist in principle.

But we are faced with a more substantial problem with respect to corporate bodies. If a body changes its name, is it the same body with a variant form of name, or a new body altogether? Debates on this point have marked code revision since the beginnings of the recognition of corporate entry. The reason such debates have taken place is that under traditional cataloging theory, one must choose one side or the other; establishment of official headings was the guiding force. With the proposal here, no such choice need be made. A special type of link will exist that can allow either assembly or separation of the groups of publications bearing the two names, as the cataloger may desire.

On the other hand, not all the problems related to corporate entry are resolved. Corporate bodies merge, split up, spawn subdivisions whose names indicate either independence or subordination (regardless of the administrative facts). There might even be a nebular reorganization of (say) bodies A, B, C, and D into the new complex P, Q, R, T, and S. There could be problems of determining when a name denotes a body. As an illustration, "Germany" once stood for a national idea, not a corporate body, nor even a well-defined geographical area. It is hard to state when it became a corporate body or entity for subject cataloging purposes. "Catholic Church" has at times stood for a collection of more-or-less semiautonomous corporations sole, at other times for the Roman Curiae, sometimes for the corporation sole of the Pope, or the Christian church visible or invisible, etc. Just to identify the differing relationships among names, the taxonomy of links may well become complex.

Turning to personal names, the case of multiple pseudonyms has exercised catalogers through the years, primarily because of the requirement that a uniform heading be established. Is the bibliographical or biographical person more important in the establishment of personal name headings? The online catalog, as defined above, provides a way out of the dilemma. A number of names may belong to a common person. Or a number of persons may belong to a common personal name (e.g., Ellery Queen and Nicolas Bourbaki). Special types of links may be used to permit assembly or scattering of the publications by the catalog user according to the relationships among the names.

It is too easy an "out" to state that the objectives of a catalog determine whether various forms of a person's biographical identity need to be brought together in a catalog. Linking all the names used by a particular person to a common address that is in principle accessible for search has the result of making such debates meaningless even though one may still have qualms about the concepts of personal and bibliographic identity. Cataloging procedures are not metaphysical claims.

Turning to another point of collection in an alphabetical catalog, works, we are faced immediately with a concept whose very existence can be cast into doubt. Are works merely fictions created to present a desirable filing order in a file laced with the writings of voluminous authors? Or are they

Platonic forms, manifest only in printed and imperfect copies? Or something else again? In concrete terms of cataloging, they are different from texts, because the same text can be manifest in two different works, works that may even have different authors, carrying differing ascriptions of authorship. One can even imagine hierarchies of works, sub-works, editions, etc., that may or may not parallel texts, their recensions, and corrupt versions. If each work is treated as a separate address in the file, suitably linked to other works or sub-works, one can see that the online catalog would permit any of a number of useful displays, depending on the goals of the searcher.

But there is a more important problem surrounding works in a library catalog. They must have names in a catalog requiring established forms of name. The form of the established name of a work is usually that of an author-title heading, perhaps qualified by details of the edition. This type of "standard citation" is usually thought to be the last refuge of the notorious main entry. It is thought that this refuge will survive the online catalog because earlier justifications for it have revolved around the technological constraints of fixed display systems such as card catalogs. But in the online catalog as described earlier, this justification is missing. Any approach to a work should be satisfactory, as long as it has been linked to the address. The main justification, the real justification for main entry, is found in the socially organized requirements of citation. These requirements are not rationally organized; they have grown up through custom in various professions and disciplines. The various forms of citation order found in the *Chicago Manual of Style* provide impressive evidence for this claim.[4]

The arrangement of library materials that are about given people, topical subjects, or other works can be resolved. Although filing the entries for such materials by title or date of publication provides an awkward display, especially when one has a previously composed list of citations in hand, something like a filing medium resembling bibliographic citations should be available to the user of the catalog. This filing medium usually has an author first, followed by the title, and maybe some material about a given edition. Here is main entry "redivivus," but only for the function I've described. It doesn't mean that a standardized form of name has to be used, unless there is more than one book by a given author in the file being examined and the author has a variant form of name. Except for this one case, the online catalog can allow the use of the title-page form of name (the one usually prescribed by manuals of citation practice anyway) to form the author heading. The exceptional case can be provided for in any number of ways, but I suspect the usual searcher will prefer the use of the title-page form of name found either on the alphabetically earliest filed or else on the latest published title-page as the standard. It might be noted that options here will be of interest only to sophisticated searchers working their ways through very long files.

It will also be noted that a second mistake in cataloging theory manifest in previous discussions and now revealed as technologically bound to a particular form of display is the importance placed on filing rules. Only in the case just mentioned are filing rules of any type going to have any pertinence, and even there, there should be little complexity in them because of the comparatively short files under examination. On the other hand, if a library were to print its catalog out into some fixed medium, filing rules would become important.

Throughout the above discussion the terms "link" and "address" have been used. An address is best described as a common identity, and is known only by the forms of name it has and the other addresses linked to it in various, specified ways. In this way, an address resembles a Leibnizian monad, describable only by its relations to other monads.

Various kinds of address can be seen as authors as persons, authors as "bibliographical entities," etc. Note that the works associated with a name having a bibliographical identity can be a subset of the works of a single person or writer, as well as the fact that a writer for the purposes of the catalog is but the sum total of writings entered under it in a catalog. Works can be subsets both of other works as well as works composed of other works, with even more complex combinations possible. An analogous description of corporate bodies whose names are used as addresses can be formulated.

With respect to links, I have not compiled an exhaustive classification. To do so would be to compose a code for true online cataloging. It is obvious that there are many kinds of links, all of which appear to beg for classification once enumerated. Examples of links are those between variant names of a person or corporate body, those between authors and their works, those between works, sub-works, editions, physical copies, and so on.[5]

In conclusion, two main points are to be made. The first is that although the model of an online catalog helps illuminate a general theory of cataloging, it must also be applicable to fixed forms of catalog display, the only constraints on the general theory being imposed by the technological difficulties of making a display such as that afforded by an online catalog.

The second point is that we will be able to concentrate on the real relationships between names in the catalog. The flexibility offered by the various types of link will allow catalog users to assemble only those materials they want rather than be drowned in a sea of material associated with unsought and unwanted names. They will no longer be at the mercy of cataloging rules for arbitrary decisions on what constitutes the body of material they seek.

Once the mistake on which cataloging theory rests has been corrected, quasi-philosophical problems about the nature of cataloging vanish, especially those based on a continuum of bibliographic conditions where there is no good criterion for placing a given work or name in one category or another. Although there is a metaphysical view presented in the concept of address, the concept of uniform headings, based on fixed-display catalogs, has been replaced by that of an address.

It is almost trivial to observe that librarians are working with catalogs in their present state of development rather than what should soon be available. The profession should create a new cataloging code, now, for the online age, before the database management technology for a new generation of online catalogs has finally arrived, and old ways of thinking are even more hopelessly embalmed in large files. The mistake of uniform headings is what has prevented Gorman's vision of a catalog from coming into existence. Correcting that mistake is what needs to be done.

Response to Michael Carpenter's "Does Cataloging Theory Rest on a Mistake?"

Michael Carpenter praises my paper with faint damns. The point of disagreement seems to be that he believes there is no role for the standard, "official" form of name or title in the online catalogue, whereas I believe that the importance of the role of such forms has been over-exaggerated. However, there is a course that the online catalogue can chart between the Scylla of the main entry and the Charybdis of Carpenterian chaos. One can only have respect for anyone who describes anything as a "Liebnizian monad" and still more for someone that can use a $1,000 phrase like that in the context of cataloguing. I suspect that each of our visions of the future of cataloguing has its own validity and, sadly, that neither has the faintest chance of becoming a reality.—*Michael Gorman*

Notes

1. See his "Cataloging and the New Technologies" in Maurice J. Freedman and S. Michael Malinconico, eds., *The Nature and Future of the Catalog: Proceedings of the ALA's Information Science and Automation Division's 1975 and 1977 Institutes on the Catalog* (Phoenix, Ariz.: Oryx Press, 1979), 127–52; the main paper is also

reprinted in Michael Carpenter and Elaine Svenonius, eds., *Foundations of Cataloging: A Sourcebook* (Littleton, Colo.: Libraries Unlimited, 1985), 242–52.

2. "Statement of Principles" section 5.2 in International Conference on Cataloguing Principles, 1961, Paris. *Report.* Reprint ed. (London: Clive Bingley on behalf of IFLA, 1969), 92. Sections 5, 6, 7, 8, 9, and 11 all use the term.

3. Gorman appears to be mistaken in stating that there will be any distinction between added entries and references. Nothing but links of various types will remain.

4. *Chicago Manual of Style,* 13th ed. (Chicago: University of Chicago Press, 1982), 440–47.

5. The links are different from the relationship enumerated by Barbara Tillett in her *Bibliographic Relationships: Toward a Conceptual Structure of Bibliographic Information Used in Cataloging* (Ph.D. diss., University of California, Los Angeles, 1987). Appendix A (pp. 280–98) contains an exhaustive list of bibliographic relationships based on an exhaustive search of library cataloging codes published since 1841. None of Tillett's relationships are between bibliographic entities and the persons and bodies producing or otherwise responsible for them.

Cataloging for the Third Millennium

Arnold S. Wajenberg

In all fairness, I must begin this response to Michael Gorman's "After AACR2R" with a confession, or at least an explanation. I first encountered Michael Gorman when I heard him speak about cataloging and the MARC format at the University of Illinois–Urbana campus. I was at once captivated by the clarity, wit, and insight that he brought to bear upon these subjects. Shortly thereafter he became director of technical services at the University of Illinois at Urbana–Champaign, and so became my colleague and my boss. Gradually, thereafter, he also became my friend. Furthermore, his views on cataloging agree with mine at least 90 percent of the time.

Consequently, this response cannot pretend to be an objective appraisal of his article. In my view, all of its major theses are obviously correct; that is, they agree with my own views. There can be no doubt that the MARC format began, and largely remains, an automated version of the 3" x 5" card. Computers are really good at manipulating data, so online catalogs should consist of related packets of data; searching, storage, and catalog maintenance are all facilitated thereby. It therefore follows that the catalog code for the era of online catalogs should guide the cataloger in the creation of such records, and something like Gorman's HYPERMARC is necessary with the MARC format incorporated into the cataloging code. Whether we will ever really have it is, of course, another question.

Rather than further elaborate what Gorman has stated so well, in this article I will discuss two environmental factors that should be taken into account in future cataloging codes: the influence of an online environment on catalog records, especially headings, and the effect of cataloging for a network as well as for an individual library. I will next discuss two specific situations that, in my opinion, receive insufficient attention in the present code, and should be given more attention in the code of the future: the cataloging of reproductions, and the distinction between published and unpublished library material.

A Code for the Online Catalog

Although filing rules have not been included in any of the cataloging codes used in the English-speaking world, these codes have all presupposed an alphabetic listing of entries in either a book or a card catalog. The alphabet has served as the organizing principle for book, card, and microform catalogs, with the exception of classified catalogs (and even they are supplemented by an alphabetic index). An online catalog may present lists in alphabetical order, but it need not be limited to this mode of display. In my ideal online catalog, the person using it should be free to specify what is displayed, and in what order. The results of a search might be listed alphabetically by author or by title, or in chronological or reverse chronological order, as specified by the searcher. It should be possible to limit the search by language, imprint data, format, location of material, or such factors as the searcher may specify. All this requires that the necessary information not only be included in the catalog record, but also encoded in such a way that a program can find it.

In such a catalog, the placement of a heading in an alphabetical sequence is relatively unimportant; what is of fundamental importance is the character string keyed in by the searcher and the ways in which the system treats that character string.

In her articles evaluating the importance of standardized headings and cross references in online catalogs, Arlene Taylor presupposes an online catalog with keyword searching of headings and automatic right-hand truncation.[1] If such features were to become standard in online catalogs, we would need rather different rules for formulating headings. AACR2 quite rightly requires that a name heading be based on the best known form of a name, and for corporate bodies gives preference to entering subordinate bodies directly under their own names, rather than as subdivisions of their parent bodies. For an online catalog as specified by Taylor, these rules should be modified. The best heading for a name will be the most complete form of the name, so long as that form includes the best known form. Why not use as the heading "Mozart, Johann Chrysostom Wolfgang Amadeus," as long as it can be retrieved by a search under any part of it, including "Mozart, Wolfgang Amadeus" and "Mozart, W. A."? In fact, with keyword searching, inversion of surnames is also unnecessary, and the treatment of Icelandic and Arabic names is greatly simplified. The rules for choice of entry-element in compound surnames and names with prefixes become unecessary.

Similarly, the rule for corporate subdivisions should require that such bodies always be entered as subdivisions of their parent bodies, and that the complete hierarchy of parent bodies be included in the heading. With keyword searching, anyone looking for one of these headings can enter a search using the name of the subdivision and as many terms from the names of parent bodies as are useful for specifying the search. For example, someone looking for publications of the agency called "Kidney Disease Branch" can enter that name directly. If there are too many agencies with that name, so that too many extraneous items are retrieved, the search could be refined by adding terms from the names of any of the parent bodies in the corporate hierarchy (subdivisions are preceded by double hyphens):

```
United States--Dept. of Health and Human
    Services--Public Health Service--Division
    of Chronic Diseases--Kidney Disease Branch
```

(The author makes no guarantee that some parent bodies have not been omitted inadvertently.) The person using the catalog need not be troubled by this cumbersome heading, nor even aware of it, but may use any part of it in the search argument.

Of course, such rules would be appropriate only for catalogs with keyword searching capability and right-hand truncation. Unfortunately, there is very little standardization in the interfaces to online catalogs, and not all have these capabilities. Until there is much more uniformity in the way online catalogs can be searched, it would be premature to change the rules.

Cataloging for a Network

As Gorman points out, it is increasingly common for libraries of all kinds and sizes to participate in networks, of which the largest is that of the OCLC Online Computer Library Center. One result of this is ever-increasing pressure to conform to national and international standards. The incentive for this conformity is of two kinds, psychological and economic. Peer pressure, though intangible, is surprisingly effective at inducing catalogers to conform to accepted standards.

Economically, a library realizes maximum benefit from participation in a network if it minimizes the extent to which records must be changed before they are used. This accounts in large part for the massive switch to Library of Congress classification (LCC) by so many libraries; they can use the LCC call number that appears on LC catalog records without further investigation.

Libraries have the same economic incentive to use headings as they are found in the Library of Congress authority file; they can then optimize their use of Library of Congress cataloging found in whichever network they use. My library's experience is that we find Library of Congress cataloging for about 60 percent of our new acquisitions. It is clearly to our advantage to conform to Library of Congress practice when formulating headings.

This can sometimes pose problems. The rules for form of headings all presuppose that the cataloger is preparing headings for the catalog of a single library. Similarly, the Library of Congress rule interpretations (LCRIs) all presuppose that the cataloger is preparing headings for the Library of Congress catalog. For example, the LCRI for adding parenthetical qualifiers to series titles instructs the cataloger not to predict a conflict. That is, the cataloger is to add a qualifier to a series title only if there is another series with the same title in the Library of Congress catalog. If there is no conflict, no qualifier is added. What is a cataloger in another library to do if it is necessary to make an added entry under a series heading that the Library of Congress has established without qualifier, but the local catalog has a heading for another series with the same title? The library's policy is to use Library of Congress headings when they are available, and if the library uses OCLC, it is expected to follow Library of Congress for the headings it adds to the online union catalog. In my library, the solution is to revise the heading used in our local catalog. This is not usually too burdensome, because ours is an online catalog with an authority file that is interactive with the bibliographic file, so that we can revise the heading in the authority file, and all bibliographic records that use the heading are automatically corrected. However, it is not so easy to clear up the corresponding conflict in OCLC's online union catalog. It does not have an interactive authority file. If headings are to be corrected, each bibliographic record with the incorrect or obsolete heading must be changed, and this can only be accomplished by mailing instructions to OCLC's Online Database Quality Control Section. I hope readers will not be shocked at my confession that we just don't bother; we leave the mess in OCLC.

The cataloging code for the third millennium should rise above the parochial emphasis on the local catalog. It should provide instructions for preparing headings for a national online union authority file, and eventually for an international equivalent. The local authority file should simply be a subset of the union authority file. Fortunately, the basis for moving in this direction already exists, in the Name Authority Cooperative Project (NACO) initiated by the Library of Congress. In this program, a number of libraries contribute name authority records to the Library of Congress online name authority file. If they could begin to resolve conflicts, not only in the Library of Congress online catalog, but in such massive online union catalogs as those of OCLC and the Research Libraries Information Network (RLIN), the Library of Congress online name authority file could begin to be transformed into a national union authority file.

Cataloging Unpublished Material

The majority of the items acquired and cataloged by a library are publications: books, sound recordings, periodicals, viderorecordings, and many other types of material. However, many libraries also sometimes acquire unpublished items. AACR2 accommodates unpublished textual material by providing a chapter for the description of manuscripts. In the 1988 revision, the code begins to recognize that every type of material may exist in both published and unpublished forms, by providing rules 1.4C8, 1.4D8, and 1.4F9–1.4F10. These rules instruct the cataloger that for unpublished items, only date of production, which is substituted for a date of publication, is appropriate information to record about manufacture and dissemination of the item.

However, adequate cataloging of unpublished material, and especially archival collections of such material, requires more detailed guidance than these brief rules provide. Perhaps each chapter in Part I needs a supplement for unpublished material; perhaps the rules could be generalized into a supplement to chapter 1 for unpublished material. A beginning has been made in this direction by some special cataloging communities, which have produced manuals for both archival and graphic materials.[2]

Another requirement for the adequate cataloging of archival collections is a rule prescribing an access point under the heading for the person or corporate body that is the focus of a collection of unpublished materials that is being described as a unit. Such a collection may consist of manuscripts, but it may also be made up of any other format, or a mix of formats. The collection may include many items that are not authored by the person, or do not emanate from the corporate body. Nevertheless, the person or body will often provide the most important means of finding the catalog record for the collection.[3]

Cataloging Reproductions

It seems quite certain that the present concern with the preservation of deteriorating library materials will continue well into the third millennium. The reproduction of such materials is likely to remain an important means of preserving them, and therefore the provision of bibliographic control for both the originals and their various reproductions will continue to grow in importance. The instructions in AACR2 for cataloging reproductions are quite adequate for individual libraries, but they do not work so well in a network environment. The problem is already acute for serials. A search for a serial title in a database such as the OCLC online union catalog can retrieve a bewildering array of responses, including cataloging for the original serial and for various kinds of reproductions of various parts of it. As a result, a meeting sponsored by the Library of Congress, called the "Multiple Versions Forum," recommended a two-tier hierarchical model for the description of serials, with the description of the original given in the online union catalog, and the details about the various reproductions given in holdings records.[4]

However, reproductions of serials make up only one of many types of reproductions that libraries now acquire. Textual monographs and printed and manuscript music are often reproduced as paper photocopies and microforms, and there is some interest in copying texts, music, and graphic materials on optical discs. Motion pictures are now routinely acquired as copies on videorecordings, of course in a variety of formats (Beta, VHS, videodisc, etc.). Old 78 rpm sound recordings may be reproduced on tape, or rereleased on 33 1/3 rpm or compact discs. Computer files from their inception have been notoriously fluid, transferring easily among tape, floppy disk, and hard disk formats, and in a baffling array of versions.

This situation cries out for Gorman's HYPERMARC records, with their interconnected packets of information. We can imagine the basic description for a motion picture consisting of a 245 field and a group of 5XX fields, giving the title, statement of responsibility, a list of the cast and significant production information, and a summary of the plot. This record would be linked to several authority records, thus providing access by means of appropriate name and subject headings. It would also be linked to several records, each consisting of a 260 field, a 300 field, and several 5XX fields, that would give publication, physical description, and supplementary information about the original motion picture and about as many different reproductions as should prove necessary. The large central online database would contain all of the related descriptive packets. Each local library could use as many of them as it needed in its local catalog. This technique could be used for any configuration of multiple versions of any format. Local catalogs would not lose any useful information, and shared networks would not be swamped by ever-increasing multitudes of nearly identical records for the same work. The cataloging code for the third millennium should provide guidance for the creation and use of such related information packets.

Conclusion

These remarks are little more than an attempt to apply the ideas in Gorman's article to some specific problems that, in my opnion, badly need to be solved. I wish I did not share his pessimism about the likelihood of our attaining what is needed. However, a millennium is a long time, and necessity may drive us in the direction we should go. Probably by 2990 most of these problems will have been solved.

Response to Arnold Wajenberg's "Cataloging for the Third Millennium"

Arnold Wajenberg's article is a perfect example of my old friend (and sometime comrade-in-arms) at his lucid and practical best. His proposal that cataloguing codes for online catalogues should take the realities of online catalogues into account could only be considered radical by the most irredeemable of cataloguing mossbacks. The idea that cataloguing for a network (in time, we hope, for The Network) should involve a move away from parochialism (one of the cataloguer's most virulent occupational diseases) is a call for a change of attitude that can only be the result of internal change rather than a mandate by a cataloguing code. His ideas on the comprehensive treatment of unpublished material should be considered and adopted by the JSC as they work on AACR2R2.—*Michael Gorman*

Notes

1. Arlene G. Taylor, "Authority Files in Online Catalogs: An Investigation of Their Value," *Cataloging and Classification Quarterly* 4, no. 1 (Spring 1984): 1–17.
2. See Steven L. Hensen, *Archives, Personal Papers, and Manuscripts: A Cataloging Manual for Archival Repositories, Historical Societies, and Manuscript Libraries,* 2d ed. (Chicago: Society of American Archivists, 1990); and, Elizabeth Betz, *Graphic Materials: Rules for Describing Original Items and Historical Collections* (Washington: Library of Congress, 1982).
3. Hensen, *Archives,* 5–6.
4. "Multiple Versions Forum Report," report from a meeting held December 6–8, 1989, Airlie, Virginia (Washington, D.C.: Network Development and MARC Standards Office, Library of Congress, 1990), 7–16.

Future Cataloging Rules and Catalog Records

Barbara B. Tillett

I would like to see a day in the future when all libraries have computerized bibliographic systems, and catalogers are assisted by knowledge-based systems. The knowledge-based systems would include interactive rules for descriptive and subject cataloging and guidelines for record creation, indexing, and display. As a cataloger prepares a bibliographic, holdings, or access control record, the cataloging rules and data entry guidelines for each data element of the record would be available as either a passive resource to consult on demand or an interactive check on the data entered. That day is technically possible now, but would benefit from changes in cataloging rules and changes in the MARC formats for bibliographic, authority, and holdings records.

I have a slightly different view of what future bibliographic records would look like than does Gorman, but I agree with him about the need for a substantial change to the MARC format in order to progress towards more sophisticated bibliographic access tools. I also agree with him about the need for cataloging manuals that incorporate rules with specific guidance for record creation.

Cataloging rules typically have been based on the practical problem-solving experience of large libraries dealing with ever growing catalogs. Rules tend to reflect an accumulation of experience and an application of guiding principles rather than resting upon an empirical basis. This is not all bad, as long as we constantly review our old experiences in light of changes in the bibliographic world and update our approaches to take advantage of the innovations and opportunities new technologies may offer. Of course, continued empirical research would be most welcome, and should be incorporated into future cataloging rules.

Gorman has suggested what might be attempted in a next revision of AACR2. I agree that it would be very helpful not only to eliminate some of the Western ethnocentricities and to change some of the holdover practices from the days of typesetting book catalogs, but also to simplify the entire issue of uniform titles. On this latter point, I feel there is a great deal of work to be done to rethink the principle of basing a bibliographic record on the "work" in the Lubetzky sense of the abstract intellectual content. The principle of "title page sanctity" should instead hold for the description and not be cluttered with the conflicting principle of basing description on the "work." A link to the "work" is provided through an access point, which in my view should be given secondary status and used for arranging displays of records. The current rules are needlessly elaborate for a filing device meant to improve the arrangement of large files. We can link the bibliographic description of an item to an access control record for the work to accomplish collocation of all manifestations of a work, which is the function of this filing device. We also need to review the principle of describing the piece in hand, which I would slightly modify to recognize not only that we are describing the piece in hand but also equivalent items. This may be accomplished within a single multilevel record or through a group of linked records (such as the proposed hierarchically related "multiple versions" records).

In addition to the changes in the rules Gorman suggests, I would also add an introductory section giving basic principles and guiding concepts upon which we have built library catalogs and will continue to build bibliographic systems.

Those basic principles and guiding concepts should be stated clearly at the start of a set of rules to help us keep them firmly in mind. For example, we have the concept of "title page sanctity" or preserving information as we find it on the chief source of information and augmenting it as needed for clarification. We describe the item we have in hand (or in the case of some computer files, the item we know exists and can be accessed in our library, even if we don't physically have it in hand). We have a "rule of 3," which is very useful in book and card catalogs to avoid lengthy and numerous entries and to sort out "important" access points and elements of description. Is the rule still useful in computer-based bibliographic systems?

We also have the principle of authorship, which gave us the main entry and makes access and display of bibliographic records by author of primary importance. We also have Charles A. Cutter's and later Seymour Lubetzky's finding and gathering objectives of a catalog, which lead us to identify uniquely each bibliographic item and to control the form of names, titles, and subjects used as access points in order to gather together records sharing those access points.[1]

Another guiding concept is the International Standard Bibliographic Description (ISBD). We should continue to include in our rules this well-thought-out international standard for presenting descriptive bibliographic information. ISBD specifies the descriptive data elements and the order of those data elements to include in an internationally standardized bibliographic record. We still will need that guidance, regardless of the form future catalogs may take. Several online catalogs now on the market rearrange the data elements in a bibliographic record, causing confusion from one system to the next. Let us convince those who develop these systems to use the standard.

ISBD's prescribed punctuation should be included in the rules, but described in a section devoted to display and arrangement of bibliographic records. Regardless of the format of the catalog, ISBD punctuation is useful in catalog displays to clearly delineate descriptive data elements and to facilitate understanding of bibliographic information regardless of the language of the description. However, a cataloger in the online environment need not add such punctuation, but rather it should be provided by the future MARC format, as I will discuss later.

We also have the obligation to identify bibliographic relationships, to indicate to users of our catalogs related editions, other manifestations, and related works. We have created devices for accessing bibliographic information, linking bibliographic records, and identifying bibliographic relationships, but many of those devices evolved from the technologies available to us at the time.[2] Computer technology has now given us an opportunity for creative approaches to improve description and access.

Before we take those creative approaches, we should have firmly in place an AACR3 that transcends the format we use to communicate or store bibliographic information. AACR3 might be constructed as follows:

an initial section on principles and cataloging concepts for
    bibliographic description and access;
general rules for description, essentially like those in the present
    AACR2R;

a section on access, indicating the essential and desirable points of access to a bibliographic record (e.g., provide access by author, title, subjects, series, etc.) with a continued indication of the primary access (i.e., main entry) based on the principle of authorship (we still need this to order displays and arrange bibliographic records on screens and in indexes, and to provide citations for related bibliographic materials). This section also would describe the creation of each type of access "package" (to use Gorman's term);

a section guiding the construction of displays of bibliographic records (e.g., start the entry with the principal author's name followed by the ISBD structured description, using ISBD's prescribed punctuation). We also need here to clarify a standardized arrangement of multiple bibliographic records, another "ISBD," an International Standard Bibliographic Display.

Such a set of rules is important to document existing practice, but I then would use that basic set of rules to create customized cataloging manuals for individual libraries. I do not mean customized in the sense of changing the rules for local practices, but rather identifying the subset of rules in the internationally accepted set of rules that pertain to the types of materials in the library's collections. This subset of rules would be augmented by guidelines for record creation appropriate to the technology available to the library. For example, information on creation of catalog cards would be included for those libraries not in the computer networks. For those in the computer networks, inputting standards and guidelines would be included for record creation. The customized cataloging manual would incorporate not only the descriptive cataloging rules, but also rules and principles for subject analysis (classification and subject headings) and guidelines for display of bibliographic information (format of bibliographic records and arrangement of multiple records).

This would mean several "manifestations" of the rules for libraries creating machine-readable records and those that do not create such records. A common element would be the descriptive cataloging rules from the basic set of rules, covering ISBD data elements, their order in a bibliographic record, and rules for access and display. Customized cataloging manuals directed towards book and card catalogs would include information on displaying the records in book format (such as used in national bibliographies) or card format (which will continue to be used in many libraries). For example, the rules for description also would include the rules on providing ISBD punctuation, since such catalogers would need to apply the punctuation as they provide the description. Customized cataloging manuals directed towards libraries with online catalogs would be something like the "HYPERMARC manual" Gorman proposed for the creation of machine-readable records, but in an online interactive format. The rules for ISBD punctuation in this customized manual would be left to the section on displays, because such punctuation would be provided through display constants associated with the "MARC III" coding (further described below).

I agree with Gorman about the need for substantial change to the MARC format in order to progress towards more sophisticated bibliographic access tools. However, I also think we can use the existing MARC formats (and future format integration) as we develop more sophisticated systems. The MARC format is just the means of communicating data, and as long as we include specific coding that clearly delineates that data, we can manipulate it for retrieval and display. We have developed MARC formats for biblio-graphic records, authority records, and holdings records. I would like to see us continue to evolve those records into interrelated bibliographic records, access control records, and local holdings records.

The interrelated bibliographic records in the future "MARC III" format would at first glance look similar to present-day MARC records, with an adjustment of the tags to correspond to the ISBD areas of description. However, they would be records for description and subject analysis and not have the familiar access fields (1XX, 7XX, 8XX), but instead have "marked" descriptive text for data requiring controlled access. With a knowledge-based conversion system, we should be able to map existing MARC fields into the new structure and appropriately "mark" text for access. We would also add linking information for those records that are bibliographically related, in many cases using traditional linking devices, such as notes, with a nontraditional connection to the related bibliographic record(s). An example of nontraditional connections might be found in the generation beyond HyperText links or "buttons" that would not only connect but clarify available paths for users to reach their destination in the catalog's records, such as through specifying the relationship paths to derivative works, whole-part relationships, sequential relationships, etc.[3] Some of that linking could be done by a knowledge-based conversion system. My Ph.D. research indicates that linking information for bibliographic relationships would be needed for about 75 percent of the total database, and much of the linking requires human judgment.[4] It won't happen quickly, but neither has our present conversion effort to get records into machine-readable form.

We would need a new means of marking text in bibliographic records for information that is intended to have controlled access, such as names, series, and some titles of works. This might be similar to the blocking techniques now used for word processing or in HyperText programs. The subject heading fields would by default have controlled access (unless they were intended to be uncontrolled). Controlled data elements would be connected automatically to related access control records for those subjects.

Picture the "MARC III" format for bibliographic description records as follows:

0XX *linking information* to related bibliographic records and holding records, plus *coded information* pertaining to the description of the item being cataloged (language, geographic area, etc.), that is, the existing 0XX MARC fields, minus the standard numbers (which now would be 8XX) and classification numbers (which now would be 9XX)

1XX *title and statement of responsibility information,* with marked text for information requiring controlled access (e.g., authors' names, the title of the work represented) with primary authorship indicated by imbedded coding of the marked text

2XX *edition statement,* with marked text for information requiring controlled access

3XX *material specific details*

4XX *imprint,* with marked text for information requiring controlled access (e.g., publisher's name)[5]

5XX *collation* (physical extent, illustration, size, etc.), possibly with marked text for types of illustrations

6XX *series statement,* with marked text for information requiring controlled access

7XX *notes,* with marked text for information requiring controlled access

8XX *standard numbers* (ISBN, ISSN, LCCN, SuDocs number, etc.)

9XX *subject analysis* (classification, subject headings, etc.), with marked text for information requiring controlled access. The classification may also appear in related holdings records as item-specific call numbers.

ISBD punctuation would be omitted for data entry and instead moved to display constants associated with specific MARC field and subfield coding, that is, supplied for display purposes based on the MARC codes. This would demand a clearer coding of such subfields as parallel titles, which currently reside in the same subfield as other title information.

The "MARC III" format for bibliographic records could be used for hierarchically related bibliographic records, such as those for different physical forms of items deemed to be copies of the same manifestation of a work. In this configuration, interrelated bibliographic records, whether related hierarchically or having other bibliographic relationships, would be linked for display capabilities. The hierarchically related records would be displayed in a form similar to the old "dashed-on" entry format, which could still be used when the record was displayed in a card format. Other types of relationships might be indicated with traditional linking devices or, in an online system, more sophisticated pathways could be presented to the user as options to continue the search.

In addition to the "MARC III" bibliographic record format, we would also have a "MARC III" format for access control records, which would be connected to the "marked" text in the bibliographic records. These access control records, like present-day authority records for names, titles, or subjects, would include related entities and variant forms of names, titles, or subjects, indicating the predominant or chosen form to prefer as a default for access. That is, a default form would be indicated to collocate records sharing that name, title, or subject, when no particular form was selected by the user. However, another form could be chosen as a preferred form by the user of the bibliographic system, as desired.

A third "MARC III" format, in addition to those for bibliographic records and access control records, would be for holdings records. Such records would be linked to the appropriate bibliographic record and include an item-specific call number, including the item's location at a specific library and its location within the library, volume and copy information, local barcode information, and item-specific notes. Holdings records for most materials would rarely be communicated beyond the local library or a regional union catalog, but might be viewed remotely by a user querying the library's catalog from anywhere in the world. There would be exceptional cases for communicating local holdings information to a national resource database, such as for preservation master copies and display of serials holdings for interlibrary loan purposes.

These three types of "MARC III" records would allow us to link records or provide ways for users of online systems to discover the relationships and interconnections inherent in bibliographic information and those accidental, incidental, or perhaps even mystical relationships that derive from sharing an attribute (such as the same author, the same language, the same year and country of publication, etc.). We have found these latter relationships very useful in the online environment to help limit our searches and to enhance the usefulness of the catalog. Relationships among bibliographic records could also be used to interconnect a library's records for materials it owns with other records in the bibliographic universe. Access to that bibliographic universe is increasingly available to all library users.

But what about libraries that continue book and card catalogs? They will continue the linking devices used in those types of catalogs, that is, references, added entries, uniform titles, notes, etc. Any machine-readable bibliographic records used for descriptions, associated access records, and location and holdings records will continue to be able to be manipulated to generate catalog cards, COM catalogs, or book catalogs, but will offer expanded utility in the online environment. Just as libraries slowly abandoned inventory lists on scrolls for book catalogs and later abandoned the book catalogs for card catalogs in order to enjoy the increased utility of the new technology of card production, we will likewise progress and make the best use of new technologies of the future.

We should, however, remember that rules for constructing a bibliographic record should remain the same, regardless of how minimal or complete the record is or in what format it is presented. We still follow the same rules whether we have a very brief bibliographic description or description plus the full text of an item (the full text merely becomes associated with the "contents" field). The cataloging rules and principles should transcend the format we use to communicate or store the bibliographic information. There should be underlying constants for cataloging records regardless of the package we put them in.

I wish we could instantly get to the future MARC and future cataloging tools by means of a revolution. I would be among the first to join, if I thought it really could happen. But instead, I am more optimistic about a slow evolution where we keep in mind a clear direction for improvement.

Response to Barbara Tillett's
"Future Cataloging Rules and Catalog Records"

I have the greatest respect for Barbara Tillett's work in the area of authority records in online systems. I suspect that the differences between us are largely matters of semantics and emphasis. She agrees with me that MARC (1) should be replaced and (2) will not be replaced. She takes a somewhat more sanguine view than I on the possibilities for progress through revising MARC and its applications. Her proposed "MARC III" (more properly, I suspect, "MARC II.V") certainly looks workable but fails to stir this aging bibliographic radical's blood. As the immortal P. G. Wodehouse observed in a very different context, "A hellhound is always a hellhound, whichever way you slice him." MARC sliced, rearranged, and garnished will still be MARC, and its flaws will continue to haunt our work.—*Michael Gorman*

Notes

1. Charles A. Cutter, *Rules for a Dictionary Catalog,* 4th ed., rewritten (Washington, D.C.: Government Printing Office, 1904), 8. Seymour Lubetzky, *Principles of Cataloging* (Los Angeles, Calif.: Institute of Library Research, University of California, 1969), 14.
2. For further explanation of the evolution of linking devices, see Barbara B. Tillett, *Bibliographic Relationships: Toward a Conceptual Structure of Bibliographic Information Used in Cataloging* (Ph.D. diss., University of California, Los Angeles, 1987), 84–121.
3. Further description of bibliographic relationships can be found in Tillett, *Bibliographic Relationships,* especially the taxonomy of bibliographic relationships, pp. 24–25.
4. Tillett, *Bibliographic Relationships,* 190.
5. This idea of controlling the form of publisher's name would result from elevating the data element to a potential access point. This idea deserves further discussion.

The Future of the *Anglo-American Cataloguing Rules:* A Response

Sheila S. Intner

Hurrah! Main entry is dead! Long live retrieval! There is no prediction more welcome to my ears than Michael Gorman's pronouncement that in the not-too-distant future main entry will wither away and disappear. Well, perhaps there is just one other little prediction I would embrace more warmly—the demise of the *Anglo-American Cataloguing Rules* as we know them today. For, while I agree with Gorman that they are the best rules ever devised thus far, I believe they suffer from two fatal maladies: (1) artificial separation of materials according to a set of outmoded media groupings; and (2) a deadly penchant for enumerating all possible cases for classes of data. If these diseases are not rooted out of the code successfully, I predict that AACR will come to a swift and ignominious end. The AACR we know now is a caterpillar wrapped in a chrysalis of MARC content designators. The question is, will the butterfly that lurks somewhere within ever emerge?

The Media Groupings of AACR

Charles A. Cutter's *Rules for a Dictionary Catalog* and other Anglo-American codes of that period assumed that libraries would be made up of books and the rules for making bibliographic records needed to reflect just that one type of material. (Printed serials, of course, defied control at that time, and still do.) This idea persisted into the 1950s, when the radical notion that cataloging rules should deal with other kinds of manifestations emerged.

Then, the Library of Congress, accustomed to dealing with music, films, and other nonbook media, offered guidance for United States librarians by publishing the rules it used to catalog them.[1] But it was not until the first *Anglo-American Cataloging Rules* in 1967 that rules for describing such oddities were incorporated into the same code with the rules for books. The first edition of the *Anglo-American Cataloging Rules* (AACR1) combined rules for various nonbook media groups into Part III, separating them from the description of book-related media in Part II. Altogether AACR1 had ten chapters for specific types of materials. Individual types of media broke down as follows:

chapter 6, books
chapter 7, serials
chapter 8, incunabula
chapter 9, reproductions
chapter 10, manuscripts
chapter 11, maps, atlases, etc.
chapter 12, motion pictures, filmstrips
chapter 13, music
chapter 14, phonorecordings
chapter 15, pictures, designs, 2-D representations

The 1978 second edition of the *Anglo-American Cataloguing Rules* (AACR2) made important revisions to the order and definition of the media groups, which its successor, the 1988 revision (AACR2R) did not alter. Currently, they are as follows:

chapter 2, books, pamphlets, printed sheets
chapter 3, cartographic materials
chapter 4, manuscripts
chapter 5, music
chapter 6, sound recordings
chapter 7, motion pictures and videorecordings
chapter 8, graphic materials
chapter 9, computer files
chapter 10, three-dimensional artefacts and realia
chapter 11, microforms
chapter 12, serials

Progress in the grouping of formats, aside from the purely cosmetic changes (e.g., sound recordings for phonorecords, graphic materials for pictures, designs . . ., etc.), and the rearrangement of chapters, involved four basic differences:

1. putting incunabula with books, and filmstrips with two-dimensional pictorial materials, whether film-based or not;
2. splitting AACR1's two rules for microform and photographic reproductions, and giving the former a chapter of its own, but making the latter the last set of rules in the first, general chapter;
3. adding videorecordings to motion pictures to create a new grouping based on the ability to represent the appearance of motion; and
4. creating new chapters for computer files (called "machine-readable data files" in 1978) and three-dimensional materials.

Interestingly, the changes did not happen all at once. Between 1967 and 1978, chapters 6 (1974), 12 (1975), and 14 (1976) were revised and issued separately. The revisions in chapters 6 and 14 added ISBD punctuation and incorporated already agreed-upon minor changes. But, in response to pleas from practitioners, chapter 12 was augmented to include a host of new audiovisual media commonly collected by school and public libraries. The name of the chapter was changed to "Audiovisual Media and Special Instructional Materials."

With the publication of revised chapter 12, videorecordings, charts, dioramas, flash cards, games, kits, microscope slides, models, and realia appeared as totally new media, and slides and transparencies joined the crowd, bidding good-bye to their chapter 15 cousins.[2] The only medium left out of the bulging audiovisual chapter was computer material, then called machine-readable, because the rule-makers felt the developing rules were not ready for publication. Between 1975 and 1978, this happy amalgam of materials was divided, again, into the chapters shown above for the second edition. These divisions remain in force at this writing, although indications are that there are chinks in the armor, i.e., the easy, clear-cut application of various chapters to items being collected by libraries and the smooth functioning of the rules within those chapters to the materials being cataloged.

Question: Is there any reason to expect that information storage technologies will remain static, supporting indefinite retention of the AACR2/AACR2R divisions?

Answer: No.

Some, including this writer, believe they have evolved already to the point where AACR2R's divisions no longer work. Where, for instance, do music videos properly belong? What will become of interactive video, which combines computer hardware and software with videodiscs and, possibly, facsimile reproductions? Is it fair to ask catalogers to use three or four chapters of AACR simultaneously, dealing with conflicts on a case-by-case basis? This strategy might seem to work, but it tends to create, over time, a patchwork of disparate solutions to problems that are not seen to be related until the solutions themselves create new conflicts. Haven't we had enough of this crazy quilt of quick fixes? Wouldn't we be better served by a different strategy—a strategy that assumes physical formats are not cast in stone and solutions to problems must be generally applicable, transcending particular media groupings?

And speaking of physical formats, how shall we deal with computer-based reproductions of text, maps, and other media? If we in the United States follow the model of microforms and disregard the rules, ignoring items in hand and cataloging instead imagined books or maps of interest to the information seeker, the future is bleak, indeed. (The situation of microform cataloging cannot be blamed on AACR2, however; it is the creature of academic research librarians who refused to accept that the reality of items in hand might deserve a higher priority than the original documents they represented.)

Cataloging by Enumeration

Beyond the issue of media groupings lies the problem of enumeration. Classifiers know that there are two ways to identify the instances in which a rule applies: We can enumerate each and every possible case, or we can establish the set of characteristics that define relevance, and be free to judge whether they apply to individual cases. (Oddly, United States librarians are not often entrusted with the right to make such determinations, since all standard United States classification and indexing tools are enumerative. One cannot help but wonder whether there are reasons this pattern has dominated cataloging over the last 125 years.) AACR2R rules such as 2.5C2, which lists nine kinds of illustrative materials that can be named in the physical description area of books, and 8.5B1, which lists nineteen acceptable specific material designations for graphics, and all other rules that prescribe similar lists of terms should be abolished in favor of rules that allow catalogers to use their judgment in selecting appropriate terminology for the items they are describing.[3] (Perhaps it is no surprise that people who once championed the North American list of general material designations now find it sorely limited, even with several additions since 1978, and rules tied to it are equally limiting.)

Can't catalogers be trusted to name physical media appropriately? How earth-shattering would it be if they differed on some terms? Wouldn't someone understand that "1 phonorecord" or "1 audiorecording" is the same as "1 sound recording"? What awful trauma would result from naming "photographs," a type of illustration not now on the list of nine, in physical descriptions along with any other kind of illustrative matter the cataloger thinks is important? Aren't library users more interested these days in the presence of photographs than, say, coats of arms? If catalogers were not restricted by past visions of what is important to information seekers, library users could benefit from catalogers' abilities to respond flexibly to their interests.

In describing materials, catalogers should use common terminology in current usage, and change it when changes in usage seem to indicate the need. The stubborn adherence of AACR's rulemakers to "machine-readable data files" when they were faced with a world that said and understood "computer software" is a case in point. Even though it was clear that computer-based materials were no longer restricted to data files and that a general material designation beginning with the word "computer" was desirable for librarians as well as lay users of the catalog, the change took many years of heavy lobbying and countless meetings of task forces and committees, to say nothing of the efforts of individuals to determine the best possible course of action.[4]

One term likely to cause problems soon is the British general material designation "multimedia." The British use it to mean any item made up of two or more components in two or more media, i.e., the type of item North American librarians call "kit." Now, however, multimedia is being used widely in government, industry, and academia to refer to combinations of computer and video items, with or without other bells and whistles. The fact is that librarians other than descriptive catalogers rarely use AACR2R's terminology or understand catalogers' adherence to it. It poses a barrier to intraprofessional understanding as well as to effective communication be- tween librarians and laypeople.

In a similar vein, subrules that enumerate exception after exception to a rule need to be eliminated in favor of simply following the general rule. Take, for example, the element of statement of responsibility. After stating clearly and unequivocally that statements of responsibility should be given in the catalog record if the responsible persons and/or bodies are named prominently on the item, and that they should be transcribed in the form in which they appear there, no fewer than fourteen subrules follow, offering qualifications and exceptions to the rule.[5] Can't catalogers be trusted to determine when something appears? Can't they determine what constitutes prominence? What harm is done if I interpret something as being prominent that my neighbor thinks is not? Supposing we did not have the qualifying subrules that say, among other things,

> don't supply statements of responsibility that do not appear, or that do not appear prominently;
>
> do rearrange the elements of title and statement of responsibility if they appear in reverse order;
>
> don't name more than the first person if a kind of responsibility is shared among more than three persons or bodies;
>
> do transcribe statements of responsibility in the order in which they appear, but, mostly, don't include titles (the anti-title subrule has four exceptions in which titles are transcribed);
>
> do supply identifying terms if the relationships of those responsible are not clear;
>
> do make notes to explain yourself if you cannot transcribe what actually appears; etc.?

Couldn't catalogers be free to use their judgment to include in the record or exclude from it, with or without titles, whatever statements of responsibility they believe will be useful? Suppose catalogers were not told not to supply missing statements of responsibility? What problem would occur if they supplied them (in square brackets, of course)? Is it not more likely that problems might occur when we give less information than would be useful rather than more? Should we use the cryptic instructions of AACR2R's qualifying subrules, or should we follow the main rule, which seems to make perfectly good sense exactly the way it is written? Perhaps the only subrule needed here is one that offers guidance in dealing with multiple parallel titles and statements of responsibility, but even it seems rather obvious if one thinks about the alternatives.

Out of the Chrysalis: Format Integration for AACR

I suggest we need format integration for the AACR2R every bit as much as we have needed it for the MARC formats. Chapter 1 of the code should be augmented to include *all* general rules, and exceptions should be eliminated insofar as possible. Reiterations of general rules in the chapters for specific media groups can be omitted, saving paper and the time it takes to flip back and forth between chapters, while subsequent chapters can be limited to the few truly necessary special rules for format-specific elements. Only two of these come to mind: material specific details and physical descriptions. Latitude should be given to catalogers to interpret and apply the principles of the code, and trivial exceptions by medium should be shunned. The three library associations then could publish two versions of AACR: a full version, which could be used for all material formats; and complete subsets of rules to be used by catalogers who handle nothing but videorecordings, sound recordings, or whatever, including all relevant general rules, plus special rules used solely for the desired medium; and a complete set of examples derived solely from materials in that medium.

With format integration, individual media would not require artificial grouping. Each medium could be treated in its own mini-chapter, with frequent, speedily accomplished revisions to rules governing material-specific details and physical descriptions in order to accommodate ongoing technological advances. Videorecordings would not have to be lumped together with motion pictures, nor would music videos or interactive videos have to be combined with them, either. Each could have individual treatment according to the dictates of the medium.

In addition, the rules of AACR must be simplified. At the moment, human catalogers find them out of control, and the potential of developing expert systems to take over the time-consuming, tedious, and costly chores of describing materials provides an especially powerful motivation for simpli-fication. To succeed, cataloging rules would have to be analyzed into a series of yes-no choices (which ought to be possible, even if it is only to enable human catalogers to use them consistently), and the software would have to account for variations in the formulation and appearance of titles, names, etc. Perhaps the rise of electronic text distribution with accompanying cataloging will prod the publishing community into standardizing the pre-sentation of bibliographic data on traditionally formatted products as well. With or without standardization of title pages and title page analogs, however, I doubt computers using simplified rules can do a worse job of uniform description than human catalogers have been able to do with the twisted mass of complications currently embodied in AACR2R.

At this writing, it is nearly fifty years since Andrew Osborn called for a few simple principles in place of an ever-growing mountain of legalistic rules.[6] Instead of seeking the simpler solutions he recommended, descriptive catalogers have 677 pages of legislated instructions—more than any previous cataloging code—augmented by more pages of precedent-setting policies established by the Library of Congress and other national libraries. Isn't it time we tried another way? Isn't it time we made simplification one of the primary objectives of code revision? Isn't it time we began practicing what we preach—namely, the exercise of logic, consistency, and uniformity?

The combination of format integration and rule simplification could transform the AACR from the obnoxious caterpillar it is at the moment into a butterfly, admired alike by those who study and follow it and those who merely observe it at work. The MARC template, with its chrysalis of content designators, encloses the familiar caterpillar, but it, also, is undergoing its own format integration. Could MARC format integration have a wider impact and a more beneficial influence than we expect? Can it impel the metamorphosis of AACR into a more beautiful form? Is it possible to hope for a new, improved code to emerge, an AACR3 that sheds the useless remnants of main entry, format separation, and rulemaking-by-exception, in one glorious bound upward toward the light?

Response to Sheila Intner's
"The Future of the Anglo-American Cataloguing Rules: A Response"

Sheila Intner believes that AACR in its present manifestation (AACR2R) suffers from two fatal maladies. (I think "chronic," rather than "fatal," is the correct diagnostic term since, even if one agrees with her, the diseases will, in the end, weaken rather than kill AACR.) These two illnesses, separation of descriptive rules by form and over-elaboration, are both curable. The first is, in my view, not really an illness at all. Most of the symptoms to which Intner points are readily resolvable and problems in application rather than incurable structural flaws. In many ways, one of the strengths of the ISBD structure is that, given the possibility of using two or more chapters of Part I of AACR2, it really should not matter which one you choose. The second malady, overelaboration and enumeration, is real and a case for radical rule-ectomy. Given a PC and a month, I could (and would, if anyone would use the result) produce a slimmed and lovely AACR2 that would be completely free of the baroque nonsense and redundancy with which AACR2 is plagued. Thus, I am prescribing minor medication for one ailment (which, to extend the metaphor, I believe to be psychosomatic) and major surgery for the real disease.—*Michael Gorman*

Notes

1. These include the following supplements to the Library of Congress's *Rules for Descriptive Cataloging in the Library of Congress,* available to the rulemakers in various draft, preliminary, and regular editions: Manuscripts (1954), Motion Pictures and Filmstrips (1965), Phonorecords (1964), and Pictures, Designs, and Other Two-Dimensional Representations (1959).
2. Formerly cataloged only if they represented single pictorial works, slides and transparencies now could be cataloged singly or in groups regardless of their contents.
3. *Anglo-American Cataloguing Rules,* 2d ed., 1988 revision (Chicago: American Library Association, 1988), 77, 209–10 (hereafter cited as *AACR2R*).
4. Nancy B. Olson gives a brief history of this and other issues involved in the expansion of AACR's rules to accommodate microcomputer-based materials in "History of Organizing Microcomputer Software," in Sheila S. Intner and Jane Anne Hannigan, eds., *The Library Microcomputer Environment: Management Issues* (Phoenix, Ariz.: Oryx Press, 1988), 22–34. Today, Olson estimates it takes a minimum of two years to obtain a rule revision, and most proposed revisions take a great deal longer.
5. *AACR2R,* 24–29.
6. Andrew Osborn, "The Crisis in Cataloging," *Library Quarterly* 11 (Oct. 1941): 393–411.

After AACR2R: My Version
of the Vision

Pat Thomas

When I was invited to contribute to this publication it was with the expectation that my comments would be a response to Michael Gorman's paper. My vision for the future differs from his. I would prefer, therefore, to make my comments more positive and less negative by presenting my own viewpoint. Actually we don't disagree so much as we view the same subject from different perspectives.

To be asked to peer into the future should be great fun, and it is in that spirit that I record these remarks. I do not have a crystal ball, nor do I claim to have a direct line to the Great Cataloger in the Sky, but on the other hand I always have an opinion and am usually willing to express it. I might add that I base my opinions on a certain amount of appreciation, not scholarly, of cataloging theory and, perhaps more importantly, on practical experience.

I stand in awe of cataloging codifiers and editors. To be able to express with precision the minutiae of detail required of a code for descriptive cataloging defies human imagination. I admire its complex concepts and structure, but I would run screaming into the night if I were to undertake an assignment such as editing AACR2R. Though the introduction of AACR in 1967 did not solve every problem or meet every need, it presented a doorway of possibilities never before opened for the cataloger. Its potential was immediately recognized by the cataloging community, and thus began the process of continuous revision. The timing of the original publication was interesting. It was early, before the age of electronic blitz and media explosion. Consequently it provided, in my view, a solid foundation upon which to build. Much of the necessary revision to the original AACR code can be attributed to the fact that libraries began to acquire nonprint materials in ever-increasing quantity and variety, and the concept of an integrated catalog was born.

I cannot envision my existence in a paperless society. I am not ready to start my day without a cup of coffee and a newspaper. Nor am I ready to curl up and enjoy a novel seated in front of a computer monitor. I can't lug my CD-ROM into the forest to sit under a tree and contemplate nature while reading poetry. For one thing, my eyesight is too fragile to risk many added hours of screen displays. What good would it do to have total analysis through complete and detailed bibliographic control if you cannot have access to the information to be found, unless that item itself is in a usable form? And I currently consider "full text" systems to be unusable.

For the foreseeable future my world still includes libraries with books and magazines and audiocassettes and CDs and videos that I can take home to enjoy for a stated period and then return. I see no reason why some of these same materials, plus lots more, cannot also be found in an academic or a research collection. And I see no reason why the same bibliographic description cannot suffice in any setting or in any milieu if it described essentially different copies of the same item. The form of the catalog really should be of no consequence as far as the description is concerned. Put another way, the item should be identifiable from the bibliographic description be it in an online catalog, a card catalog, or a CD-ROM product.

In short, I am unwilling to give up small or medium-sized public libraries. Their size is suitable for the community they serve; enlarging them is impractical or inappropriate. Increasing and expanding their resources, either material or human, by networking, increased efficiencies, or sharing is both possible and desirable. Many of these libraries are not automated, nor would a complex and sophisticated automated system be feasible given the limitations of their resources. AACR2 is the answer to a cataloger's dream for those who work in smaller libraries. At last we are presented with a code delineating standards that can be followed to produce a record far superior to what was previously possible. If the cataloger is working on and contributing to a bibliographic utility, the importance of that code is multiplied because of the shared aspect of contributed copy.

And while considering small libraries and their needs and concerns, one must include the nature or form of their catalogs. It is true that AACR2 and the MARC format and ISBD all are so closely intertwined and interdependent that they can scarcely be separated. I agree with Gorman that MARC was modeled on the catalog card; it is an electronic catalog card, if you will. It has served us well, enabling many libraries to automate to a greater or lesser degree. As such, we cannot yet afford to write it off; its usefulness is far from over. In 1989–90 OCLC alone produced 94 million catalog cards for its users. Admittedly, that number is down 11 percent from the previous year, but it is still too significant a number to dismiss the catalog card as extinct.

The MARC format is still evolving. On the one hand, format integration is imminent, while on the other hand, the MARC format for authorities has been introduced and work proceeds on a MARC format for classification. On the plus side, MARC contributes to standardization, which in turn contributes to sharing and communication in the automated environment. It is true that originally the MARC format was the vehicle used to produce catalog cards electronically. However, it has proved more versatile than its origins might indicate. It can be used to describe many kinds of materials, and machines can manipulate the bibliographic information to change the display to meet the needs of the user. In the automated system of the library in which I work, a single MARC database is used, but records display differently in the acquisitions module, the circulation system, the public access catalog, and the keyword-indexed module. By using enhanced software we can manipulate information held within the MARC record, but heretofore untapped, to sort, display, report, or print selected records. I grant you that MARC is primitive and unsophisticated. As bibliographic control evolves, MARC must keep pace. But that should not frighten one off. I believe that standard MARC records can be enhanced, changed, massaged, and manipulated to the degree required by an advancing concept of bibliographic needs. So far I look upon MARC as a blessing, not as a limiting or inhibiting factor to realizing future possibilities.

I am not against progress; my vision of the future is not constricted by my clinging to outdated concepts or vehicles that belong in the junkyard. On the other hand, I don't want to be steamrollered into oblivion by those unwilling to listen to some voices of experience. I can give up the concept of main entry just by changing all 1XX fields to 7XX. By doing so, I lose no access; I merely use a machine to manipulate the data in the variable fields in order to achieve the desired result in a screen display. No big deal. That is just one example of what Gorman refers to as detritus carried over from previous codes. Please, however, don't let huge research or academic libraries smother their smaller brothers and sisters just because they consider themselves to be more important and the needs of their smaller counterparts to be of lesser significance. Live and let live. Beyond these modest admissions of the need for change and improvement I am unwilling to go; I favor evolution over revolution. Ever the optimist, I do believe we are making progress in our march toward the future. As long as we learn from our experience and use common sense to reach our common goals, I believe that future looks bright. I would even go so far as to propose a battle cry, "One of these days, we're gonna get organized!"

Response to Pat Thomas's "After AACR2R: My Version of the Vision"

Since Pat Thomas is not responding to my paper, I shall not respond to her nonresponse. Like her, I see a future of libraries full of books and other documents, a future in which we will need cataloguing codes of some kind to make those documents available to as many people as possible. This is a humble, unexciting, and utilitarian view, and what, in the name of Panizzi, is wrong with that? We must cultivate our gardens and make the best of what the future brings.—*Michael Gorman*

Index